IMAGES
of America

LONG BRANCH
PEOPLE AND PLACES

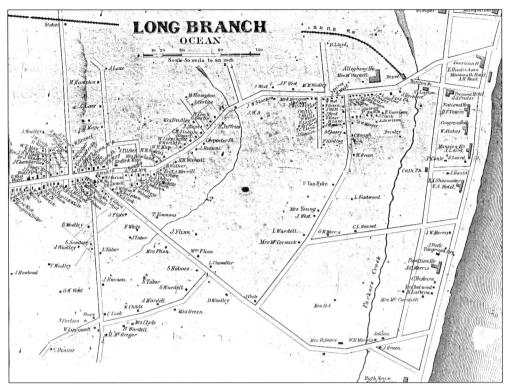

Hotels outnumbered houses in the large scale Long Branch inset on the 1860 Beers sheet map of Monmouth County. Illustrations of some, made only a few years later, can be found herein. The future city was then part of Ocean Township. Its uptown and downtown business districts were by then well formed along Broadway, the major east-west thoroughfare, known earlier as Main Street. The sides of the triangle at left are Norwood and Bath Avenues, connected by Westwood. Bath, at its eastern end, formed a north-south triangle that still exists today. Note the first railroad, approaching town from the west, reaching a Broadway depot. The shore line was 5 years in the future, the New York and Long Branch, 15 years. Parkers Creek appeared to be a well-formed stream. One wonders if its course can be traced today, perhaps along a path of wet basements.

Cover photo: see page 121.

IMAGES
of America

LONG BRANCH
PEOPLE AND PLACES

Randall Gabrielan

ARCADIA

Published by Arcadia Publishing,
an imprint of Tempus Publishing, Inc.
2 Cumberland Street
Charleston, SC 29401

Printed in Great Britain.

Library of Congress Catalog Card Number: 98-87873

For all general information contact Arcadia Publishing at:
Telephone 843-853-2070
Fax 843-853-0044
E-Mail arcadia@charleston.net

For customer service and orders:
Toll-Free 1-888-313-BOOK

Visit us on the internet at http://www.arcadiaimages.com

This book is dedicated to Wesley V. Banse of Manasquan, seen with his wife Grace, a former resident of Long Branch, who has spent decades studying, collecting, and sharing with the public the history of the Monmouth shore. Wes is a modest man, who prefers the spotlight on his publications and programs rather than himself. Having recently retired from his appointed historian's position, he is finally receiving the acclaim his output so richly justifies. This dedication salutes the man and his work in recognition of a long and meritorious career.

CONTENTS

ACKNOWLEDGMENTS

This book is the product of numerous lenders whose pictures made its publication possible. Several of these lenders merit special thanks, including Aileen Connolly, who was my earliest supporter in this project. Elene Dwyer was of great help, not only for the number of images she provided, but for her enthusiasm and interest. Gloria Hennessey's custodianship of the collection of her late husband, Daniel, a skilled photographer, is also appreciated. Gail Hunton of the Monmouth County Park System hired me to work on the Long Branch section of the Monmouth County Historic Sites Inventory, my first opportunity to explore in depth Long Branch's history. The interest grows steadily with this opportunity to explore the special meaning Long Branch has to Monmouth County. Terry and Martin McCue showed their understanding of the importance of families to town history through their crucial and meaningful images.

Tova Navarra's photography has repeatedly graced my work. I am pleased and thankful to have been given her art for this book. John Rhody, always at the fore of my projects, provided important images for this one per his consistent and exemplary practice. Kathy Dorn Severini and Photography Unlimited by Dorn's once again have demonstrated that their vintage photograph collection outside Red Bank has their famed richness and depth which should make then a starting point for all Monmouth pictorial projects. Glenn Vogel was in the vanguard of those appreciating Long Branch history and imagery. His loans for this work were extraordinary.

Thanks to all of the lenders of images, including Wesley V. Banse, Olga Boeckel, Kenneth Curchin, Mae Hoffman Fisher, Gail Gannon, W. Edmund Kemble, the Long Branch Public Library, Kathleen McGrath, Monroe Marx, George Moss, Rutgers University Libraries Special Collections & Archives, Karen L. Schnitzspahn, Robert Schoeffling, Sisters of St. Joseph of Peace, Robert W. Speck of Deal, Michael Steinhorn, Marion Wardell, Keith Wells, Marilyn Willis, and Elizabeth Wurst. Another thank you goes to Blair Hearth for the contribution of historical material and Gerald Eisner for the loan of an important and helpful series of maps.

INTRODUCTION

The challenge of a Long Branch picture history is fitting the rich and varied past of one of Monmouth County's greatest historic places into 120 pages of illustrations. Long Branch was a colonial-era oceanfront retreat, located near New York and Philadelphia when ships were the only practical means of distant travel. The absence of imagery and the sparseness of documentary and contemporary evidence leave that chapter of Long Branch's history sketchy. That era awaits discovery and knowledge in greater depth than the brief remarks in Ellis's *History of Monmouth County*.

Long Branch developed into a nationally significant resort in the first half of the 19th century; it was arguably the most prominent by 1860. Thomas Gordon's *Gazetteer of New Jersey* spoke glowingly in 1834 of its inducements to travel, "Good accommodations, obliging hosts, a clean and high shore, with a gently shelving beach, a fine prospect seaward, enlivened by the countless vessels passing to and from New York, excellent fishing on the banks, three or four miles at sea, good gunning and the great attraction of all watering places, much and changing fashionable company."

The hotels and places of accommodation by mid-19th century were well mapped and outlined. Images of many of them exist in an extraordinary collection published in J.H. Schenck's 1868 *Album of Long Branch: A Series of Photographic Views with Letter-Press Sketches*, a work from which this book draws liberally.

Presidential cachet, "the presence," and investment by industrial-financial magnates and gambling opened a new chapter in the quarter century or so from 1870. Racing at Monmouth Park and gaming houses created an unreal prosperity as more hotels were built. Long Branch was the most important place on the New Jersey shore.

Many of Long Branch's prominent visitors sought a permanent presence, building summer homes or cottages. The word should be used without quotations or amazement, as definition 6 of cottage in the O.E.D. is simply "a temporary home." This period in the 4th quarter of the 19th century coincided with the development of the Shingle Style and Colonial Revival, a period of Long Branch's importance in the history of American domestic architecture.

The hollowness of gambling-generated prosperity was demonstrated following the 1893 legislative outlawing of gambling. Long Branch, which achieved governmental independence from Ocean Township as a commission in 1867 and incorporated as a city in 1903, fell into a period of decline lasting several years into the new century. Hotels closed; some were lost. The city was dotted with properties that had become shabby.

Long Branch, maintaining a premier locale on the shore, competed with other coast towns for the vacationist trade. However, the absence of gambling cost the city its special allure. Many hotels were lost in the early 1900s to destruction or neglect. Its golden age was gone, but the shore endured. Despite the overall decline in the number of hotels, new ones were even built on occasion.

Long Branch, minus gambling and forced to develop alternate support, became a business and manufacturing center. The number of its factories increased significantly in the first decade of this century. The city was for some while Monmouth County's most populous municipality. Its numbers were channeled into political power; Long Branch was for a spell the center of Monmouth County political power.

Post-World War II Long Branch, subject to the same perils that visited many of the older resorts nearer the cities, also faced the challenge of urban stress. An improved state and national road network sent land travelers to distant destinations and made city vacationists permanent residents in new, nearby suburban developments. Low cost, fast air travel put exotic overseas places within reach, at additional expense to the local beach and hotel industry. Manufacturing has been on a steady decline throughout the older, northeast states and the local political climate provided yet another challenge.

The past cannot be re-invented, but the shore environment that made Long Branch great still provides a sparkling setting for contemporary living, recreation, and hospitality. One hopes Long Branch's future will be as bright as its past.

The Book's Organization

Long Branch's importance, the breadth of its historical career, and its vast pictorial resources made image editing a challenge. A large number of photographs were winnowed into this collection. The initial accumulation included many pictures I wish could have fit, but it was absent subjects meriting inclusion. The goal was portrayal of all sections of the city over a lengthy span. I shall accept the responsibility for any shortcomings, but also the credit if readers think the desired goal was reached. To meet my perception of balance, many fine 1860s Pach photographs were omitted in order to present glimpses of the recent past and other pictures that were simply fun.

There have been second acts for most of my Arcadia projects. The remedy of failure to portray is a second volume, presuming this one is a success. I am eager to continue Long Branch's pictorial presentation and seek picture loans for a proposed Volume II. Please contact me at 71 Fish Hawk Drive, Middletown, New Jersey, 07748. (732) 671-2645.

One

NORTHERN NEIGHBORHOODS

NORTH LONG BRANCH, BRANCHPORT, AND PLEASURE BAY

Price's Hotel, founded in 1854 and operated by the family for its 99-year existence, was located on the north side of Port au Peck Avenue, immediately off the Pleasure Bay Bridge. It served a large excursion clientele, initially appealing to them with elaborate, costly shore dinners and later clambakes. Price's, a restaurant only in its later years, was closed because of fire in 1953. This c. 1945 photograph was taken by Ed Kemble.

The *Pleasure Bay*, a 150-foot vessel built in Upper Nyack, New York, was an early steamboat used by Thomas Patten, who acquired it *c.* 1890. His steamer lines had various corporate names, but were known collectively to the public as the Patten Line. Fierce competition with the Merchants Steamboat Line resulted in Patten assuming the Shrewsbury River run, while the Merchants boats sailed the Navesink.

The amusement park on the south shore of the meeting of the South Shrewsbury River and Branchport Creek attracted many day-trippers. *Harper's Monthly* described the drive from Long Branch in 1876 as going "through a lovely open country, to an old-fashioned, original tavern in the midst of a green grove on the bank of a placid sheet of water. [Its] flavor of combined Bohemianism and rustic simplicity . . . contrasts delightfully with the ostentation and luxury of the sea-side hotel . . . " This image was taken *c.* 1905. (Collection of Glenn Vogel.)

10

Pleasure Bay Park, Long Branch, N. J.

The Patten Line and the Atlantic Coast Electric Railway built jointly *c.* 1898 Riverside Park and the Riverside Hotel. This image from a *c.* 1905 postcard identified as "Pleasure Bay Park" is presumably the same one that included a picnic grove, dance pavilion, merry-go-round, and various amusement games. The area on the South Shrewsbury River—Branchport Creek serves as housing today.

Pleasure Bay in winter, seen in a *c.* 1905 postcard image, was home to ice boating. Local waters were important in advancing the sport. Long Branch boaters developed a great rivalry with their Red Bank counterparts. The boats are classed by sail area. The one at right appears to be a Class A, the largest, with 350 square feet, typically divided between the main and jib sails at 300 and 50 square feet, respectively.

11

The founding of amusement parks by transportation companies was a typical late 19th- and early 20th-century venture, an effort to build off-peak travel hour traffic. The floating theater in Pleasure Bay Park, with a seating capacity of about 2,000, was a favorite site, where Gilbert & Sullivan operettas played among other fare.

With few surviving details, this undated early 20th-century photograph presents another star attraction. Note that horses also appear in the image at top.

The New York Hotel was built in 1867 by Isaac P. Cooper, a former operator of ocean shore hotels, on the shore of Branchport Creek, west of the route of the bridge that was later built and is pictured at bottom. The Italianate-style box, claiming a capacity of 100 guests, had an observatory affording a view for many miles. The place was renamed River Side House c. 1873. This lower priced alternative near the ocean was also a fine shell-fishing region. The hotel disappeared at an unspecified date. Housing fills the area now. (Schenck *Album of Long Branch*.)

The Pleasure Bay area, seen from the air c. 1932, has undergone two transformations. A resort-excursion area was built in the mid-19th century from a region called "Sheep Pen," as local lore claims sheep farmers brought their animals here for an annual washing. The second was post-1960 after the last hotel burned (p.14) and the area became entirely residential. The hotels are seen east or to the right of the bridge. Oceanport is north of the water, a place near the meeting of the South Shrewsbury River and Branchport Creek. The oval is Wardell Circle, now a fully built street.

Old-timers reminisce about days of yore as the end of Price's Hotel neared in 1953. Thomas Frazier Price, the last owner, is in the center, while his nephew, Edward Green, is at right. The third man is unidentified. (Special Collections & Archives, Rutgers University Libraries.)

The old Pleasure Bay Bridge, seen in a 1950s image, was located a few feet north of the present span. Today, one notices the roadway curving to the south to a fixed span as one travels in the direction of Long Branch, away from the layout of this low elevation swing bridge's route. (Special Collections & Archives, Rutgers University Libraries.)

This image appears to be a c. 1965 construction scene at the Pleasure Bay Bridge. The new, 25-foot-high span opened on September 2, 1965. New housing was later built north of Port au Peck Avenue. (The Dorn's Collection.)

In 1859, M.M. Vandyke, a New York hotel owner, built a summer house called "River View" on 8 acres bordering Branchport Creek. This fine Italianate dwelling was one of the most elaborate houses of its time in the area. This c. 1910 postcard labels it "Seaside Home, Branchport NJ," but its locale was the Oceanport side of the creek, just east of Branchport Avenue. New housing is now on the site. (Collection of John Rhody.)

The Seaman Boat Works, established in 1879 by William A. Seaman at 491 Atlantic Avenue, built a variety of craft, but was best known for its Sea Bright Skiff. The Seaman Boat Works output included the original *Fox* (see opposite), larger river launches, and a steering mechanism for military use.

The Thomas G. Patten house, a *c.* 1890s Shingle Style house was vacant and in disrepair when taken over by the Patten Point Yacht Club in 1964. Seen in this 1979 image, the place has been finely refurbished and adapted for a clubhouse on their 4.5-acre Patten Avenue lot at the mouth of Manahassett Creek. The club was an outgrowth of the Monmouth Power Boat Association; their early efforts were spearheaded by Dr. Martin Rush of Red Bank.

Seated in a replica of *The Fox* are Francis Frame, left, and Don Godshall of the Long Branch Ice Boat and Yacht Club. The original craft was rowed across the Atlantic Ocean in 1896 by George Harbo and Frank Samuelsen (see the author's *Atlantic Highlands*, p. 83, Arcadia, 1996). The club undertook the project as a result of a 1974 request from the Smithsonian Institution to Harold "Pappy" Seaman, who helped construct the original at age 13. Ten members rowed in shifts from Pleasure Bay to Mystic Seaport, Connecticut, completing their five-day trip on July 8, 1975.

The deft strokes of artist Tova Navarra's pen reflect the quietude of winter at Patten Point.

The Kingsley House, a smaller hotel at 495 Patten Avenue, is viewed on a c. 1910 photographic postcard. The figures are presumably guests, but it is not certain if all three structures are part of a hotel complex. (Collection of Glenn Vogel.)

Branchport, an important early riverfront dock for the Long Branch area, developed hotels for a commercial and excursion trade. This c. 1911 postcard looks south across Branchport Creek, likely from the Seaside Home (p.15). The Hotel Garrison, at left facing Atlantic Avenue, was gone prior to 1940, as is the pavilion in center. The Hotel Norwood, Branchport Avenue, is recognizable in its present state as a restaurant. Its porch was enclosed, the chimney is gone, and much of its detailing was removed. These private houses still stand on the block north of Kingsley Street; their changes are minor. (Collection of Glenn Vogel.)

This *c.* 1950 aerial provides a guide to several images appearing elsewhere in this chapter. The railroad right of way is the wide band through the center. Notice that the tracks are gone. The old Ocean Avenue curves at right, intersecting with Atlantic Avenue. Both sides of its first block are illustrated on p. 22. Near the top are the Asbury M.E. Church, with steeply pitched roof and square tower, and the North Long Branch School, the large building with a one-story section east of its two-story addition, both seen on p. 27.

An early Long Branch railroad station, on a spur of the Raritan & Delaware Bay Railroad, was located between Seaview and Cooper Avenues in the path of today's Ocean Avenue. That road was announced to be a line to southern New Jersey, but was built as a subterfuge in an attempt to break the Camden & Amboy Railroad's monopoly on the New York and Philadelphia route. The ensuing litigation impaired the R&DB's finances and business. In addition, access to this rail route was dependent on a steamer trip from New York to an often inadequate pier at Port Monmouth. (Schenck *Album of Long Branch*.)

The North Long Branch station, located at Atlantic Avenue and the present Ocean Boulevard, was built as part of the Long Branch & Seashore Railroad that ran from Sandy Hook to Long Branch as an opposition line to the R&DB Railroad prior to both being absorbed into the Central Railroad of New Jersey. This station, seen on a c. 1905 postcard, appears to be a c. 1890s replacement of an earlier structure. Rail service ended in 1947, but the station stood vacant for some years prior to demolition.

Daniel I. Hennessey Sr., longtime station agent at North Long Branch, is seen here at his desk in the interior of an early 20th-century railroad station.

Daniel I. Hennessey is in front of a quartet outside the North Long Branch station and appears to include a baggage handler, the hackman, and an unidentified figure waiting, perhaps for the train.

There was a significant fishing industry in northern Long Branch that also encompassed today's Monmouth Beach. Rugged, capacious Jersey skiffs were launched from the beach and drawn ashore by horses. Hennessey had two Long Branch stores about the time of this *c.* 1910 postcard, one at 63 Ocean Avenue and the West End store at 94 Brighton Avenue. (Collection of John Rhody.)

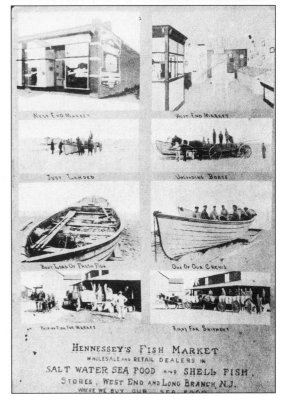

Atlantic Avenue looking west from the old Ocean Avenue is readily recognizable. The three houses on the right are still standing, although the oldest, the side-gabled place, is run-down. The 1890 *Sanborn Atlas* indicates that the front-gabled building at right, number 9, was a shelter for babies. See the picture below for a closer view of the south side. Both images are from *c.* 1905 postcards.

The first two buildings of the south side of Atlantic Avenue are intact, the post office now occupied by Bruno's Barber Shop and its neighbor, number 20, by a surf shop. The Edgar A. West Building (see p. 30), a full two-story, four bay store, appears to have a wide facade in front of a smaller building. The new Ocean Boulevard, built over the railroad right of way, creates a major break in the line of buildings.

Atlantic Avenue looking east on a c. 1910 postcard, east of West Street, reflects the higher state of preservation of the streets west of the former rail line. The illustrated houses are present, although with changed detailing. Number 82, partially seen at right, is missing its porch, while number 80 is sided and absent its brackets and porch balusters. The three houses beyond are recognizable, amid growing and obscuring trees.

The traditional-style house at 59 Columbia Avenue, perhaps dating from the third quarter of the 19th century, is symbolic of the older, smaller residences serving the local population in the maritime district. The fence and chimney are gone, while the exterior was re-shingled and sided, but the place is still readily recognizable.

The house at left still stands on the northwest corner of Atlantic and the old Ocean Avenue, its roof altered considerably. The two closer houses on the east side of Ocean are gone, but numbers 469, 465, and 459 in the background stand, with a frame multiple dwelling on the corner beyond. The image is a c. 1910 postcard.

This old Ocean Avenue scene facing north on a c. 1940 postcard is located south of the view at top. A concrete wall now separates the street and beach. This spot is near the beach maintained by the USO in the 1940s.

Mannahassett Hotel, Monmouth Beach, N. J.

The Manahasset Park Association surveyed in 1894 a tract around Valentine Street, Monmouth Beach, which also embraced the Manahasset Bay Long Branch shore between Bay and Long Branch Avenues, north of Colonia Drive. The two sections were connected by a bridge that was demolished c. 1962. The hotel, in Long Branch just north of the bridge, seen on a c. 1905 postcard, was destroyed, probably by fire in the 1930s. Regarding the description on the card, the first lecture on Evaluating History 101 should warn against believing everything printed on postcards. (Collection of Michael Steinhorn.)

"Ladies Must Wear Bathing Caps in Pool" was a prevailing rule in 1950 at the White Sands Casino, although younger readers may ask, "What's a bathing cap?" The youthful bathers appear to be taking diving instructions, beginning with little leaps at poolside. The viewers appear to have spent ample time in the sun. The City of Long Branch bought the club c. 1974 and had been operating it at a loss when it was extensively damaged by fire May 4, 1978.

Oliver Byron Engine Company Number 5 was organized as Company Number 3 in 1890; their 17 charter members included some of the best-known names in the area, including Hennessey, Lockwood, West, and White. They reorganized as Company Number 5. The crowd is unidentified in this c. 1900 image, and also large, the company had a membership of 60 in 1909.

The Byron firehouse at 46 Atlantic Avenue is seen in both images, this one c. 1950 showing changes to the door and windows. The company is named for financial benefactor Oliver Byron, a well-known dramatic actor who owned several houses in North Long Branch and Monmouth Beach.

The Romanesque Revival Asbury M.E. Church, 61 Atlantic Avenue, was built in 1894 and designed by Charles W. Bolton of Philadelphia; it replaced a frame 1872 edifice once on the south side of Atlantic. An extension built in 1898, post-dating this image, fits harmoniously. The top of the tower was removed *c.* 1945 in a rebuilding project to correct serious structural problems. The original state of the North Long Branch School is at the right.

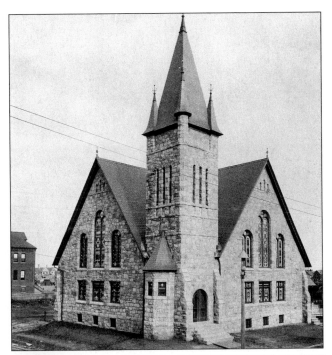

The Romanesque Revival North Long Branch School, a twin of the Broadway School, was built in 1891 at 469 Church Street, by C.V.N. Wilson, whose name appears on its plaque, and Garrett Hennessey, who is named on the building contract. That contract specified it was to be erected according to plans "submitted by the building committee," perhaps a reuse of the Broadway School's plans. The school was expanded in 1900 and again in 1929, the latter following fire damage, and closed in June 1978. The Long Branch Historical Association is planning a restoration of the vacant building to be used as a historical museum.

The Evangeline by the Sea was one of North Long Branch's larger, older hotels. It was demolished c. 1980s and is seen here in a c. 1930 image. (Collection of Glenn Vogel.)

The Avenel Boulevard curve along Ocean Avenue separates the former Reservation from the North Long Branch beach club, as seen in the summer of 1952. It was destroyed by fire c. 1960s. (The Dorn's Collection.)

Nate Salsbury, born 1845 in Rockport, Illinois and owner of Buffalo Bill's Wild West Show, bought the Liberty Street house of Frank Meader, a member of his troupe. He built a colony of about ten houses near the ocean, giving them Native American names, calling the group the Reservation. Intended as a summer home for his show, it is possible William Cody visited, but there is no evidence he owned property in Long Branch. The lone survivor, Navaho Lodge, was moved in 1983 from the east side of Ocean Avenue, north of Joline Avenue, to the northwest corner of Seven Presidents Park. This photograph shows the house receiving a new foundation that year.

Production and then storage of gas had taken place in Long Branch since at least the 1880s in various forms by different companies. The last storage tank, taken down by New Jersey Natural Gas Company in 1982, is not missed.

The North Long Branch railroad station and a number of structures were demolished in August of 1980 to prepare for the new Ocean Boulevard.

Ocean Avenue north of Long Branch, a straight road along the narrow peninsula barrier beach of Sea Bright-Monmouth Beach, once curved to the east to follow the shore at North Long Branch. A new Ocean Avenue, seen under construction in 1982, accelerated north-south travel and, in conjunction with that decade's building boom, facilitated the change of character of much of the North Long Branch shore to occupancy by multiple dwellings, including many high-rise condominiums.

Two

INLAND SECTIONS
DOWNTOWN, UPTOWN, AROUND TOWN, AND HOLLYWOOD

The Ku Klux Klan, associated with a number of Monmouth County locales, made an impact on Long Branch through ownership of nearby Elkwood Park. Their presence in the 1920s began a decline in Long Branch's Jewish population, from which the city never recovered. They also stirred fear in the Catholic and black communities. Paraders of the cowardly and hateful organization hid behind their white hoods, unaware that distinctive shoes "unmasked" some of them to observant spectators. This south side of Broadway image was taken c. 1925. The street east of Memorial Parkway is extensively changed and barely recognizable.

This Broadway scene looking west from inside Second Avenue appears to be a pre-1905 image as the minor decorative details visible on the Steinbach Building appear to make it the older store.

Broadway is seen looking east from the corner of Third Avenue *c.* 1911. The frame Rothschild Building on the south side was replaced by the present brick Brent Good Building *c.* 1915. Most of the block has been altered or destroyed. (Collection of Glenn Vogel.)

The Steinbach Building was designed by Long Branch architect Leon Cubberley and was built in 1905 following destruction of an earlier store on January 2 of that year. Clad in brick and decorated with limestone and terra cotta, it contained its own electric generator and included a modern cash system and presumably pneumatic tubes. The store was intended to be and was the finest in the city. This view was taken in the 1940s.

The 1905 Steinbach Building, later Vogel's, was also destroyed by fire, in February of 1978. The site, including the building at the left, is now the Long Branch Learning Center of Brookdale Community College. Comparing this post-fire image with the street today reflects loss of integrity of the old exteriors with removal of finishing decoration and the construction of incompatible fronts. This scene, when compared with extant buildings, shows change.

The Arcade Hotel, founded *c.* 1870 and seen in this *c.* 1915 postcard, occupied the center of the "V" where Broadway divides at Second Avenue. The Landmark Hotel at right, built 1896, was demolished in 1995.

Broadway at Second Avenue was a vibrant retail district at the time of this mid-1950s image. A.A. Anastasia's Pharmacy, long a fixture at the "V," moved west on Broadway, closing *c.* 1970s. Fred Trovato's supermarket at 129 North Broadway at right, is now the site of an auto body shop. The pharmacy building was removed at an unspecified date. (The Dorn's Collection.)

The active business block pictured opposite is now cleared. Robert Pinsky, the nation's poet laureate, born and raised in Long Branch, has regularly connected his hometown to his poetry. This influence is evident in the tablet installed in 1997 at the Broadway Triangle, the informal name for the small park at its tip, the "V" at the juncture of Second Avenue.

The Hotel Florence at 8 North Broadway, the northwest corner of Ocean Avenue, reportedly built by Richard J. Dobbins in 1879, operated under that name for many years. It appears to have begun as a one-room deep, but tall structure, and was later expanded in the rear. The site is now a vacant grass-covered lot. (Collection of Long Branch Public Library.)

Broadway, formerly Main Street, is viewed on a c. 1905 postcard looking west from just east of Second Avenue. The partially seen Long Branch Trust Company at right was remodeled beyond recognition during the 1950s, but its rear still reminds one it is an 1880s structure. Number 180 at left appears markedly different with its new storefronts and the removal of the cornice. The Long Branch Record Building, the closest of the two four-story buildings, was restored in the 1980s. However, a solid steel door, implying storage use, blocks the building from street commerce.

Philip Schmidt founded his "New York Butcher" shop at 189 Broadway in 1887. The name was likely intended to establish confidence with a summer trade but, by the early 1900s, the probable date of this image, Schmidt was proud to claim service to a year-round clientele. He cured ham, made bologna and sausage, and cooled meat with a refrigerating plant in the basement to avoid use of ice.

Broadway's curve west of Second Avenue is still readily visible, but fewer standing, recognizable landmarks make it harder to identify this 1934 postcard image looking east. The bay windows of number 153 at left help recreate the perspective. The core of the Paramount, the more elegant of the two theaters, survives as a carpet warehouse, but its tower is gone. The Strand was demolished in the mid-1990s. The Landmark Hotel at the block's end was demolished, but the adjacent brick structures survive. A paint store is now under the no longer extant billboards.

This view of lower Broadway looking west provides a second glimpse of the Anastasia Pharmacy at 101 South Broadway. The large building on the south side of Broadway, then the Paramount, is now Siperstein's warehouse; their store is just to its east. The handsome stores on the corner of Second Avenue still stand, although number 118, the 2 1/2-story building with the elaborate gable, has obviously seen better days. The removal of the billboards is one improvement to the landscape! (The Dorn's Collection.)

St. James Protestant Episcopal Church was founded in 1854, the year the cornerstone of this board and batten Victorian Gothic edifice was laid on the south side of Broadway, west of Second Avenue, the later site of the Paramount Theater (p.37). The church was enlarged in 1865 through contributions of their summer congregation, some of whom later funded a separate shore chapel (p.117). St. James moved to its present English Gothic building at the southeast corner of Broadway and Slocum Place in 1913. (Schenck *Album of Long Branch.*)

Broadway from Slocum Avenue bisects this 1951 aerial looking east. The present St. James Episcopal Church, seen on the south side at bottom, while above it on the north side is the L-shaped Garfield-Grant Hotel (p.39). Chelsea Avenue is the wide street at right, with Star of the Sea Church (p.66) difficult to discern under the pier against the shaded street. Lower Broadway's triangle, the dog-car racing track, and Long Branch Stadium (p.85) are readily spottable, though. (The Dorn's Collection.)

The Garfield-Grant Hotel at 275 Broadway was designed in the Renaissance Revival style by New York architect William Van Alen and built in 1926 by the Amsterdam Building Company of New York. Van Alen is famous for his Chrysler Building in New York, built only four years later. This was the costliest, most elaborate of the year-round hotels and is important for the distinction of its architect and as a symbol of Long Branch's business power in the post-WW I period. The exterior is reasonably well preserved despite new storefronts, but the interior was marred in the conversion to offices. Brass stair rails and wrought iron balusters suggest a once impressive lobby. (Collection of John Rhody.)

A city group inspecting a new fire engine c. early 1950s in front of the old city hall allows a glimpse of that building, the library, prior to its later extension. The house east of it moved to the rear of city hall when Slocum donated the property, now Slocum Park and the present St. James Protestant Episcopal Church. (The Dorn's Collection.)

39

The Broadway Theater, seen *c.* 1910 on the south side of Broadway east of Memorial Parkway, was on the site of today's number 154, a building that may be an expansion of this old structure.

This *c.* 1905 postcard image of Broadway looking west focuses on Joseph Goldstein's artistically designed department store on the northwest corner of Second Avenue, a spot now occupied by a bank. Downtown's principal shopping street has been frequently illustrated. Views from different perspectives are also on the bottom of 32 and the top of 36. (Collection of Glenn Vogel.)

Number 176 Broadway was an early post office building, its identity on this *c.* 1907 postcard, one presumably changed with the 1915 opening of the building on p.71. The Romanesque-influenced store and office was quite handsome, its grade floor well balanced, with its entrance between the two stores. It retains its decorative cornice, frieze, and lintels. However, a grade floor remodeling, relocating the door to the east and making one store, is unsympathetic and has destroyed street level esthetics. A glimpse of the former New Jersey Trust Company building is at left. (Moss Archives.)

The southwest corner of Broadway and Memorial Parkway, seen in a 1957 image, reflects a time of greater financial activity in Long Branch. The New Jersey Trust Company's Classical Revival building was dismembered on the installment plan, beginning with the replacement windows and the unattractive addition shown above. The old look was obliterated in a later remodeling to make the front appear as one unit, which may have made the structure easier to board up, its present status. (The Dorn's Collection.)

Dr. Z.W. Scriven, a Broadway physician, opened his New York Store in 1867 on the south side of Broadway near Washington Street. He operated it as a "cash store," aiming to distinguish himself from competitors whose store accounts for small purchases he claimed were the bane of retailing. The "New York" in his name probably reflected the higher tone of his establishment and his goal to reach the summer crowd. (Schenck *Album of Long Branch*.)

A number of Long Branch Masonic organizations trace their history back at least to 1876, meeting at various sites. A new Classical Revival-style Masonic Temple, designed by Long Branch Mason Leon Cubberley, was built at 410 Broadway in 1925. Bowling alleys and billiard tables were among its recreational facilities, with the place serving as a United Services Organization Facility during WW II. Long Branch Masons merged with a Fair Haven group in 1980, resulting in the 1981 sale of this building, which appears not to have changed since this c. 1950s image. It is now an office. (The Dorn's Collection.)

The Broadway School was in a residential neighborhood when built by R.H. Hughes, architect unknown, in 1890, on a lot reportedly the site of a school for some time. Two additions to the Romanesque Revival-style structure, with many fine architectural details, are visible in this 1954 image of a busy commercial district. Schooling ended in June 1981. A variety of retail shops occupy the former Packard agency at the left, as Highway 36 replaced Broadway as Long Branch's automobile strip. (The Dorn's Collection.)

Arthur and Frank Siegfried purchased the vacant Broadway School for a modest $50,000, spending a considerable sum to gut the interior and remodel it for offices. The project, designed by Joseph Peters of Red Bank, maintains exterior integrity, adding an attractive entrance in the rear, while creating new space inside. Arthur, at left, and his father, Frank, are seen on the job site on May 1, 1986.

William E. Styles built this fine Italianate-style residence at 77 Grand Avenue *c.* 1870, a rare instance of a brick Long Branch house during this period, a condition giving it minor historic stature. He may have lost it because of cost, as an early deed describes a mechanics lien action. C.F. and Mary Jacobus occupied it for much of the late 19th century. The decorative lintels, tin cornice and frieze, highlighted by dark blue paint in the recent past or brick when new, are less visible with the current light gray painting.

St. Luke's organized in 1861, the successor to Methodists in Long Branch who purchased a building in 1856 that was erected as a Presbyterian church. Construction of the pictured building, designed by E.H. Finch, began in 1865. The cornerstone was laid in May 1866 and a lecture room opened for worship in January 1867, with the church completed and dedicated in July 1869. Initially named Centennary, the congregation changed the name said to be "lacking a progressive tone" in 1879. This edifice was destroyed by fire in 1893. (Schenck *Album of Long Branch*.)

The Richardsonian Romanesque-style St. Luke's Methodist Church at 535 Broadway was designed by Poole and Sutton of Newark and constructed by Randolph and Ashbel Borden of Shrewsbury, built in 1894 to replace the one shown on the bottom of p.44. Although noted diarist William R. Maps complained it was too costly, the building's substance reflected a congregation's prosperity, nearing the time Long Branch would transform itself into a business center. The scene has changed little; a large cross was added at the upper tower windows. (Collection of Glenn Vogel.)

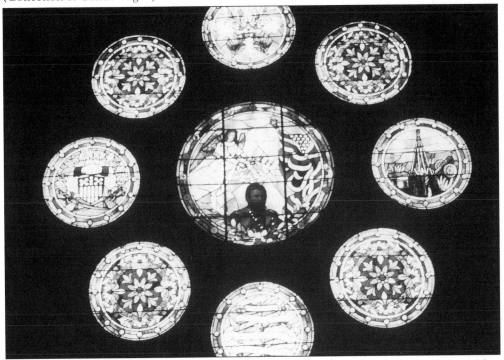

President Ulysses S. Grant worshiped at St. Luke's. His friend and Ocean Avenue neighbor George W. Childs paid for a memorial in the present St. Luke's, this Peace Window on the east wall designed and built by Century Glass Co. of Philadelphia and dedicated in 1888. Grant is seen in the center, surrounded by figures of Peace, Victory, and Mourning, and the inscription, Grant's benediction at Appomattox, "Let us have peace." Numerous artistic stained-glass windows decorate St. Luke's; they merit a visit.

Newing's Hotel was an uptown facility in the heart of Long Branch's traditional business center at 586 Broadway. It was likely taken down in the 1940s, its lot apparently part of a gas station's grounds. The image is from the early 1900s, although the place was called Finn's Hotel by 1916 (opposite). Margaret Newing owned the property in 1940.

A few constants make this February 1916 Broadway scene looking west recognizable. Grand Avenue is at right, beyond still-standing 615 Broadway. The tower of the Reformed Church is seen next to the "I." The annotator is anonymous, but lived at "II," marked "our home" on the original postcard, while "III" and "IV" were Morris Timbrook's blacksmith shop and C.V. Goodnough's shoe store. (Collection of Glenn Vogel.)

Broadway looking east in 1916 from Norwood Avenue is recognizable today by the dormered stores and dwellings, left, numbers 593–7 Broadway. The Long Branch Banking Company is denoted by the "I"; their building is better seen on the top of p. 51. The hotel on the opposite page is marked "IV," while the corner buildings were replaced by a gas station. The "II" and "III" denote the former barbershop of the annotator's father and Curtis's hat store. (Collection of Glenn Vogel.)

William Taber's pharmacy at 551 Broadway is seen *c.* 1900, a building apparently shared with a paint store. The structure may exist, as much—altered old buildings line the block today.

The intersection of Norwood Avenue, seen looking south at Broadway during an ice storm, has changed a great deal since 1916. The drugstore building was acquired by Shadow Lawn Savings & Loan, which built a modern bank on the site. A gas station is at left; the "I" indicates the former site of Curtis's hat store. The "II" denotes the Oceanic Engine Company, still there in a much altered building, but the lot in front of it is occupied by a replacement building and parking lot. (Collection of Glenn Vogel.)

The Shadow Lawn Savings and Loan Association built this stylish Art Moderne bank at the southwest corner of Broadway and Norwood Avenue c. late 1930s. It has since been expanded on both streets, c. late 1950s, with the entrance relocated to the side. However, the spacious interior benefited from the remodeling, a reminder that banks were once expansive, comfortable, and impressive structures. (The Dorn's Collection.)

The Woman's Christian Temperance Union erected a fountain memorial to Dr. Thomas G. Chattle, dedicated May 30, 1899. A local ordinance passed that month designated a 6-by-2-foot area as a park at the juncture of Broadway and Norwood Avenue. The fountain impaired modern traffic and was relocated in October 1978 to the grassy area north of the new city hall.

The uptown post office and the law offices of Wilbur A. Heisley and W.S.B. Parker are seen in this 1883 image; they are in the right and left windows respectively. Standing from left to right are: Mattias Woolley, Althea Allen, and Lewis Williams. Postal identity was a key 19th-century distinction between uptown and downtown, which were previously known as upper pole and lower pole. The Long Branch Post Office was founded in 1834, while a Branch Shore office opened in 1867 near the shore. That was changed to East Long Branch in 1873. In 1882, the shore office was changed to Long Branch, while the uptown office became Long Branch Village, then Long Branch City in 1886, and Station B in 1902, its present identity. (Collection of Long Branch Public Library.)

Upper Broadway, viewed looking east in a 1956 photograph, includes a partial view of the *c.* 1920s Long Branch Banking Company building, now occupied by Fleet Bank. The solid Classical Revival look of the bank-as-fortress has since been compromised by large windows. The commercial block east of Branchport Avenue has been marred by removal of its decorative detail and an irregular mounting of siding. Note St. Luke's at right, also on p. 45. (The Dorn's Collection.)

Neptune Hose Company Number 1, organized in 1877, a successor to Hook and Ladder Company Number 1, was housed in other companies' quarters prior to receiving a new Branchport Avenue house in 1890. This building, a 1906 vernacular Victorian design with its stone facing offering a Romanesque touch, is altered to fit functional need, while retaining its integrity. The horse fit the old opening well; modern equipment does not. An extension for a truck was built on the north and the former door was enclosed. (Moss Archives.)

Upper Broadway is viewed west from the corner of Branchport Avenue, seen on a c. 1907 postcard. The early headquarters of the Long Branch Banking Company, founded in 1872, at right, is a meeting of the Greek Revival and the Commercial Italianate. The building was replaced by the Classical Revival structure partially seen opposite. The western end of the block is largely intact, although most fronts are changed.

Painter and paper hanger A.F. Golden was the apparent owner of this still-standing 1901 Commercial Italianate building at 581 Broadway. His name and date plaque are gone, but the broken pediment cornice crest makes the structure instantly identifiable, although marred by a white painting. The subjects in this c. 1905 postcard are unidentified, but one suspects they may be owners of the respective businesses. Notice the neatly stacked barrels.

51

The First Reformed Church was substantially rebuilt in 1902 in the Romanesque Revival style, perhaps also including then the Colonial Revival alterations now present. Work included building the tower on the northeast and the large cross-gabled wing on the west, not visible in this *c.* 1910 postcard. The rectory is shingled, the work probably contemporaneous with the church remodeling. The scene, looking west, is similar today. (Collection of Glenn Vogel.)

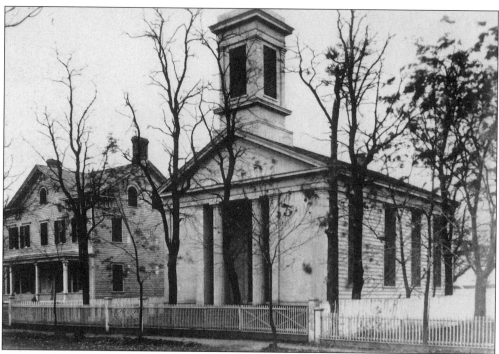

This handsome Greek Revival church was completed prior to its dedication on November 22, 1849. Their founder, Nathaniel Conklin, left the region early in 1851 while the church was organized that July. The rectory was built in 1866. (Schenck *Album of Long Branch.*)

This 1916 image is an alternate view of the scene on the top of p. 47, with the photographer having stepped across the street, condensing the view of the south side of Broadway, but providing a good look at the handsome Classical Revival building on Broadway. It is possible the sender of the series of photographic cards with Roman numerals was a baker named Gootheil. The I and II refer to bakeries, which would fit their location. (Collection of Glenn Vogel.)

The Morris Vanderveer & Company variety store, described by Schenck as "a few rods west of the Pole," (likely Broadway) had been the site of the William Green homestead. The building was occupied by Borden Morris as a furniture warehouse and dwelling until sold to John A. Morford in 1865, who moved from a nearby one-story structure he had occupied since 1835. (Schenck *Album of Long Branch*.)

Mary and Joseph Fuga appear quite pleased with their new 1928 Model A Ford as they prepared to take a celebratory drive from their Art Street home.

Joseph Fuga is seen admiring his tomato crop c. 1937. They were canned whole or made into paste. During the month of August, the tomatoes ripened at once. The raw tomatoes were dipped in hot water to remove their skins and placed in Ball jars, that were boiled to preserve the contents. A stock to last the year was typically canned; sauce was made later from the tomatoes or paste.

Mary and Joseph Fuga, c. 1937, admire, newly arrived grapes, artistically arranged, prior to wine making. The fruit was dumped in a hopper with a rotating handle for crushing to permit fermentation, a serious process timed by phases of the moon. Fermenting juice was placed in barrels to age, prior to bottling for home consumption. The remaining juice was distilled into grappa. Bottles were often buried in cellar dirt for temperature control.

O.K. Perhaps they expected the arrival of the photographer at Michael and Marie Cammarano's Bar at 609 Broadway in 1951, but his paragon of neatness deserves pictorial preservation. We all must have something we would like to see so well organized. (The Dorn's Collection.)

The New York and Long Branch Railroad opened at Long Branch July 4, 1875 to a major celebration. The line, advertised as the "all land" route to the shore, still required a short ferry ride from New York to Jersey City, but obviated the major steamer run to Port Monmouth or Sandy Hook. The Long Branch station is seen on this c. 1910 postcard absent its original tower. The line, jointly operated by the Pennsylvania Railroad and Central Railroad of New Jersey for most of its history, has been run by New Jersey Transit since January 1, 1983.

In-town gas stations are becoming scarce and mid-block pumps virtually nonexistent. The Depot Garage at 225 Third Avenue, opposite the railroad station, is boarded up. Food is still served next door at 229 and the railroad theme is repeated in the name of the Station Café. (The Dorn's Collection.)

Marvin and Edward Moses, owners of the Casey Jones Restaurant at the northeast corner of Third and Morris Avenues since 1973, sought a promotional theme and moved two boxcars and a caboose to their site in the fall of 1978, fitting the interiors for dining. The building had recently been the Long Branch Inn and earlier P. McEilany's Hotel in 1889 and the Hotel Ten Eyck in 1912. Proximity to the railroad station was the key influence for their plan, which endures 20 years later.

J.V. Durham sold fish out of his 378 Morris Avenue home, implied by the presence of the business in the 1912 Boyd's Directory, which also listed the premises as Edith Durham's residence. Little else is known about this building, which Durham bought in 1901. He died in 1916. (Collection of Glenn Vogel.)

The Central Hotel was built c. 1870s on the future Third Avenue, opposite the railroad station. It was not prosperous and was bought not long after construction by Richard P. Dobbins, a member of the Monmouth Memorial Hospital. He sold them the hotel under favorable terms in 1890. The hospital was founded as the Long Branch Hospital Association in 1887, but changed its name in a 1889 reorganization. Its beginnings were in rooms over a store and later a house. This undated image of the Second Empire-style structure is likely stylized; the impressive porch, appearing to be stone, was of frame construction.

Monmouth Memorial built two additions to the original Central Hotel, the first on the south (right) in 1899 and later on the north in 1904, the approximate date of this postcard image. The nearly identical wings are compatible with the hotel, built with mansard roofs long after they were out of fashion. The two wings were named for Tacie Harper, a board member who became superintendent in 1898 and George F. Baker for his generous benefactions. These structures were removed at an unknown date.

58

Monmouth Memorial expanded eastward planning a new central hall with two wings in 1939. The Mary Owen Borden Wing at left was built in 1940 with funds donated by Betram Borden. The Wimpfeimer Wing, not visible, connected the new and old sections. The Community Wing at right was built later and dedicated in June 1952, the two appearing to form a wide-angled "V." (The Dorn's Collection.)

Emily Sagurton of Shrewsbury, born 1907, became a Monmouth Memorial nurse, studying at the Ann May Nursing School. Dr. Ernest Fahnestock, a benefactor of Monmouth Memorial, wished her to be an operating room nurse in New York, but Emily preferred Monmouth County and marriage to James Curley. This image was taken c. 1927. Emily died in 1975.

A McCue milk pick-up truck is seen c. 1915, probably driven by Mr. Murphy. McCue typically bought milk from Upper Freehold Township where several farmers might leave their color and design-coded cans at a pick-up site. The driver checked each can for odors, typically arising from cows milked too soon after feeding, as grass or onion smells could be imparted to the product. He rejected impaired raw milk.

The McCue facility is seen in 1932, the plant at center and the loading platform to the right. The plant included a sterilizer, pasteurizer, cold storage, and bottling facilities. McCue also distributed butter and various Walker-Gordon products. They sold on an open account system, the family still proud of their record of continuing deliveries during the Depression despite lagging payments. McCue's was sold to Shore Dairy, Loch Arbour in 1962.

Martin McCue, born 1865 in Marlboro, had early experience operating a hay press and in general farming prior to purchasing a 50-quart-per-day milk route in the late 1890s. He established McCue's Dairy at 272 Willow Avenue, building it into Monmouth County's largest. McCue married Mary Stapleton of Colts Neck and the couple had three children. He was a county road superintendent, official of the Monmouth County Building and Loan Association, and member of various civic-fraternal organizations.

A decorated McCue's Dairy wagon is poised to participate in an early 1920s boardwalk parade. The event and driver are unidentified, but the three children are Mary McCue, Mary Eager, and Marlene Eager. The adult at right is Helen Manion Crook Perry, with an unidentified companion.

Dr. Thomas Green Chattle, born 1834 at Greens Pond, Warren County, was one of Long Branch's major figures of the 19th century. He was educated at Pennington Seminary, graduated Dickinson College in 1852, beginning the study of medicine in his senior year, which he completed in 1854. He became a physician and professor at Pennington in 1855, the same year he moved to Long Branch. Chattle practiced there his entire life and was active in public affairs, notably in education. A Democrat, Chattle served in the state assembly and senate. Active in the Methodist church, he married Emma A. King in 1856. She and 11 of their 13 children survived him at his death in October 1889.

Dr. Chattle led the effort to establish a high school in Long Branch; the first, dedicated in July 1876, also included primary education, typical of the times. A school devoted exclusively to secondary education was not opened until 1899, when this building, seen on a c. 1911 postcard, was erected on Morris Avenue and named for Dr. Thomas G. Chattle. It was replaced in 1927 by the present Long Branch High School. (Collection of Glenn Vogel.)

This Chattle High School graduating class, c. 1906, appears to be a studious, ambitious group. Elizabeth McCue's family preserved the picture, so she is the identified one, in the middle of the top row with the hand on her left shoulder.

The present Long Branch High School on Westwood Avenue was designed by Ernest A. Arend and built in 1927, following a long campaign to secure public approval to replace the then inadequate facility.

Long Branch High School, having established a soccer program in 1934, celebrated its 1941–2 team as its most successful to date with six wins in nine games. Coach Townley Carr is at far left, while manager Alden West is seated in front. Team members, from left to right are: (first row) Bill Speck, George Liming, co-captains David Johnson and John Golden, Bob Liming, and Frank West. (middle row) Frank DeMatz, Ralph Miller, Earl Brousell, Jules Eisenberg, Height West, Nathan Levinson, and Robert Brainard. (back row) Henry Osborne, Joe Ruscio, Tom DeLisa, Joe Cosentino, David Bernstein, and Joseph Caridi. (Collection of Robert W. Speck.)

The Long Branch High School band is seen marching in the 1975 Columbus Day parade, an event dedicated that year to the memory of Rocco N. Bonforte, Long Branch postmaster and civic leader. He originated the city's Columbus Day festivities, but died the week prior to that year's celebration. A moment of silence in his memory was observed when the parade reached the reviewing stand.

They called themselves the Flora Dora Sextet, each with a winning smile to dress up the drabness of their green, sleeveless v-neck gym suits. Seen in 1939, they are, from left to right: Gertrude Solomon Maron, Ingrid Karrberg Quirk, Theresa Fuga McCue, Hilda Karrberg Kampf, Rose Rutkowitz O'Shan, and Virginia Graham Bolton. At right are Edison E. "Ted" Bresett, legendary coach for whom the high school stadium is named, and Joe Schlenger.

Five Long Branch High School senior contestants for Miss Mardi Gras, a designation made at the annual Halloween parade and celebration, are seen in an October 1977 image in front of the school. From bottom left, they are: Mary Jo Mazzacco (the eventual winner), Carmine Ortiz, and Lynne Keenan. At top are Alicia Elmore, left, and Sharon Johnson. The bell, cast in 1876 in Troy, New York, once installed in a later-demolished elementary school, was remounted on school grounds in 1976 as part of the system's Bicentennial celebrations.

Early Roman Catholic Mass was occasionally seasonally celebrated in homes or a hotel, prior to the establishment in 1852 of the first Star of the Sea Church on the south side of Chelsea Avenue, east of the New Jersey Southern Railroad tracks. No surviving image has been located. The Stick Style second edifice, built in 1875 on the northwest corner of Second and Chelsea Avenues and designed by Jeremiah O'Rourke, was initially clapboard clad; the shingles were added later. This c. 1912 image includes the former rectory behind the church, built c. 1880 and moved when the present rectory was erected in 1915–16.

The building at top, destroyed by fire on December 5, 1926, was replaced on the same site by the present Gothic Revival stone structure designed by Robert J. Reilly of New York and erected by John P. Hallahan, Inc. of Philadelphia. Ground was broken on January 16, 1928 and although basic construction was finished in December, an incomplete interior delayed opening until May 12, 1929; the dedication followed June 9. This 1994 image reflects a newly restored and cleaned building, an extensive project designed to assure the future of a fine ecclesiastical landmark.

The Star of the Sea Academy, opened in 1885 at 152 Chelsea Avenue, was an early site of shore Catholic education. The Second Empire-style house was probably built c. 1868 by William Lane, who sold it to Daniel Dougherty, a foe of anti-Catholic bias, who sold the house to the Sisters of Charity of St. Elizabeth in 1885. Initially including primary instruction, the Academy focused on secondary education after opening of the Lyceum in 1900. An addition was designed by Vincent J. Eck and built in 1928. The school closed in the early 1970s due to declining enrollment and is vacant following occupancy as a treatment center. (Moss Archives.)

Aileen Conway Connolly, a May 1927 graduate of Star of the Sea Academy, recalls the personal education with considerable individual attention she received there. She is at left in the top row. Her classmates are, in front, Dorothy Coleman, left, and Marie Miller Marsden. To Aileen's left are Muriel Fisher Stone, Carolyn Smith Clarke, Mary Ellen Davison, Audrey Pietz Metcalf, Florence Heffernan, and Agnes Nolan.

The stone Romanesque Revival Star of the Sea Lyceum, designed by Jeremiah O'Rourke & Sons, was an elementary school built by the church in 1900 to embrace expanding enrollment in the earlier Academy. The school, located at the northeast corner of Chelsea and Third Avenues, contained a "lyceum," a second-story auditorium. An addition was built on the rear in the 1950s. The building maintained interior as well as exterior integrity over many years, including the period following closing after the 1985–86 academic year. A City of Long Branch educational facility occupies the building today. (Moss Archives.)

Sister Alicia Maria, born Mary Keenahan, 1874 in Passaic, joined the Sisters of Charity of St. Elizabeth at Convent Station in 1891 and was professed in 1894. She taught science, but could teach any subject and was placed in charge of the high school section of the Star of the Sea Academy in 1895, serving 46 years as principal. Aileen Conway Connolly recalled her as a "wonderful teacher and woman." Sr. Alicia Maria was especially helpful to those in need, whether it be with academics or personal problems.

Woolman Stokes, a hotel owner and active investor in utilities and real estate, bought the Brinley tract, choosing its home site for the 1865 construction of this Italianate-style house. It was located on Wardell Avenue, near Chelsea Avenue, a short distance from his Continental hotel. (Schenck *Album of Long Branch.*)

The sender of this 1912 postcard commented that damage was worse than depicted. Thus, perhaps a series of cards was made or the photographer chose not to photograph any of the 40 buildings reportedly destroyed. This scene is not identified.

Congregation Brothers of Israel, seeking newer quarters closer to its membership base, built a new synagogue at 250 Park Avenue in 1977. They moved their torahs to the new building in a ceremonial procession on March 27, 1977.

Baptists first worshiped at their Bath and Emmons Avenue site in 1881 in a tent, following the lot's purchase in anticipation of a church. A chapel was built in 1883, the First Baptist Church organized in 1886, but their building was destroyed by fire in March 1892. This shingled Queen Anne-style edifice was completed in 1894. It is similar in appearance today, although painted yellow. The southeast square tower faces the aforementioned corner.

John Nastasia is presumably to be the man in front of his "cash grocery," 194 Norwood Avenue, at the northwest corner of Wall Street. His use of the building exterior as a virtual billboard appears effective, albeit aesthetically obnoxious. His corner is now a piece of lawn and a parking lot. (Collection of Glenn Vogel.)

U. S. P. O. Buildin

Long Branch, N. J.

Dedicated May 31
1915

Hon. Thomas L. Slocum
Postmaster

Post Office established
1835, mail brought by
stage from Keyport,
New Jersey.

Free Delivery estab-
lished 1898, number
employes 8, 1915 staff
employes 12 clerks, 18
carriers.

The fine Georgian Revival post office at the northwest corner of Third Avenue and Van Dyke Place was designed by Oscar Wendereoth, supervising architect of the government office. Its cornerstone is dated 1914 and it was probably completed not long before the May 31, 1915 dedication date on this unusual postcard. The distinctive, artistic office reflects Long Branch's significance at that time and the influence of the Colonial Revival in Monmouth County design. There are few changes to this east facade, but an addition was built on the rear (west). (Collection of John Rhody.)

The handsome mid-19th-century farmhouse at 364 Cedar Avenue reflects an era of active Long Branch agriculture. Frederick Behr, a German immigrant, bought property in 1862 to raise flowers, later dividing it among three daughters, with one named Eisle continuing the flower business. A road-widening project threatened the vernacular house illustrated in this recent image, an event that helped uncover its history.

In a preservation story the equivalent to David's slaying of Goliath, Aileen Connolly stopped the road builders cold. The city would not or could not stop the project, so with help from only a family member, they researched the property's history and secured listing on the National Register of Historic Places in 1979. The road builders withdrew, choosing not to take on the administrative hurdles. The house had previously received a Bicentennial project Century Home plaque, that Edgar Dinkelspiel, left, presented to Aileen and her husband, Robert, in November 1975.

John Hoey, president of Adams Express Company, began building his many houses and elaborate gardens in 1863. His estate, totally hundreds of acres, was along Cedar Avenue, with the New York and Long Branch tracks, after the line was cut through his property, an eastern boundary. He called it Hollywood for its holly plants, but he transformed the grounds to a principal showplace of the eastern United States. This 1867 image is his residence, an early example of the Second Empire style. (Schenck *Album of Long Branch*.)

The Hoey carriage house and stables consisted of two buildings connected by a broad platform used for carriage maintenance and cleaning. The stable floors were laid in two-inch-thick ash and walnut, while all finishings were done in an elaborate and costly manner. The upper floor was a large billiard room. (Schenck *Album of Long Branch*.)

This 1867 view of the Hollywood lawn does not suggest the elaborateness of the plantings installed later. A principal attraction were flower gardens designed in the style of various Oriental rugs. The 1891 discovery of financial irregularities at Adams Express led to the unraveling of Hoey's finances. He died in 1892. Adams foreclosed its substantial mortgage in 1902 and the grounds were sub-divided. Private housing fills Hollywood now. (Schenck *Album of Long Branch.*)

Hoey built several houses throughout his grounds. This Stick Style house, designed by John B. Terhune and built *c.* 1866, was described by Schenck as the "Cedar Avenue house" attached to 6 acres of grounds. The observatory gave a fine view of the surrounding countryside. (Schenck *Album of Long Branch.*)

Hoey's Lodge was his principal guest house and personal quarters for winter visits when the main house was closed. The house survived through modern times at 211 Cedar Avenue as a private residence, its stature enhanced by visiting 19th-century luminaries who stayed there, but it was extensively damaged in a January 1983 fire and the remains demolished. Note the decorative carved wood stag's head, with real antlers measuring 4 feet. (Schenck *Album of Long Branch*.)

Hoey's elaborate, extensive estate brought him legions of guests. He built the Hollywood Hotel *c*. 1880 out of lumber of an abandoned Grand Excursion House. It was a building that "resembled an Oriental palace in wooden fretwork." The hotel, located at the southwest corner of Cedar and Hoey Avenues, was destroyed by fire in 1926.

The Long Branch Horse Show was organized in 1893 by the Monmouth County Open Air Horseshow Association, the last year of racing under the old system. They bought 25 acres of the Hoey estate and built this fine grandstand, seen on a *c.* 1910 postcard, and exhibition facility. The event attracted major participation in top equine circles. It continues to be held in the last week of July, but the event was moved in recent years to East Freehold Park. (Collection of John Rhody.)

A since expanded Monmouth Medical Center is at the center of this December 1962 aerial. The two vertical bands at left are the New York and Long Branch tracks, near the edge, and Third Avenue, the western boundary edge of the hospital. Second Avenue, now the eastern boundary of Monmouth Medical, is the north/south street at right, bisected by the former right of way of the Central Railroad's Shore line. Note the former gas tank at top. (The Dorn's Collection.)

Three

THE SHORE COMMUNITIES

BEACH AND SURF, WEST END, AND ELBERON

Long Branch's iron pier was one of Monmouth County's engineering marvels. It was designed by Maclay & Davis of New York, architects and engineers, and built by Job Johnson of Brooklyn. The 1878 Long Branch Pier Company had New York capital and the backing of Warren and Charles Leland, owners of the Continental Hotel, who hoped that a pier at its waterfront would improve business. The 700-foot-long pier was begun in the fall of 1878 and completed the following June. This image is from the steamer *Plymouth Rock's* 1880 trade card-time table announcing their twice-daily trips from New York for a one-way fare of 50¢ or a one-day, round-trip excursion of 60¢.

This 1879 photograph of the new pier depicts a crowd overdressed by contemporary standards and reveals the image on page 77 to be an artist's conception. A February 1880 storm damaged the center section of the pier, which was lengthened in the repair process to 872 feet. A 700-foot-long bulkhead was built on the bluff to support a promenade deck.

Storms and collisions took a heavy toll on Long Branch piers. The fifth was built in 1908, the one that survives in most 20th-century imagery. It was hoped the pier would be a major entertainment center, but a series of minor pavilions, rides, arcades, and halls lined its length over many decades. This image is from the 1920s. Note the dance hall. (Collection of Karen L. Schnitzspahn.)

Substantial structures were built near the boardwalk by the 1930s. This aerial view places the pier in the context of its surroundings, including the Chelsea Baths, behind it on the west side of Ocean Avenue. Note the Star of the Sea Church on the right edge, center, and part of the Long Branch Stadium at bottom. (Collection of Karen L. Schnitzspahn.)

The pier, lacking major entertainment, became known as the fishing pier, a designation on this 1920s postcard. A 1940s advertising card mailed when whiting and ling were running, indicated "no restriction on pier fishing" and "open night and day—every day," including the winter. The pier was substantially damaged by fire in June 1987.

The "New Era," a 1,340-ton packet built in Maine and launched in April 1854, had ill fortune on its September 19, 1854 voyage from Bremen prior to reaching waters off Long Branch. Cholera took a toll of about 40 and a storm at sea killed three. The damaged ship, blown off course by bad weather, ran aground in November near Life Saving Station Number 3. The rescue effort, involving the breaking of a line secured for a life saving car, turned into a stormy disaster. Only 132 survived; 240 drowned. This popular image is an artist's impression from a sketch made on the morning of the wreck.

The Red Sea Line steamer *Rusland* struck a submerged wreck off Elberon on March 18, 1877, while en route from Antwerp to New York. Passengers and crew totaling 204 were rescued, but the ship was a total loss.

The steamer *St. Paul*, then one of the largest in trans-Atlantic service, ran aground off Long Branch on January 24, 1896. It remained there until February 4, attracting large crowds in the interval. Excursion trains from New York and Philadelphia, as well as farmers in a variety of rigs, flooded the scene, including as estimated 20,000 on a Sunday. Food profiteers had a field day. Passengers and cargo were removed and damage was slight. (Special Collections and Archives, Rutgers University Libraries.)

The *Charles K. Buckley*, a three-masted schooner carrying lumber to her home port of Elizabethport, foundered off Long Branch on April 16, 1914, and ran aground, taking the lives of Captain J.H. Hardy, his wife and five of the crew. Only Emil Martinson survived. Life-savers' communications were tardy due to a downed telephone wire. Their efforts at firing a lifeline failed, except for the one on which Martinson was pulled to shore. The lumber cargo tossed on the waves, precluding their launching a rescue boat. (Collection of John Rhody.)

Bathhouses are seen in front of the Ocean Hotel in this 1873 image. In 1876, *Harper's Monthly* described their set-up: "At the opening of the summer season, the shore in front of each hotel at Long Branch is taken possession of by certain men of semi-seafaring appearance, who proceed to set up on the sands, just under the bluff, rows of bathing huts of an architecture so contemptible . . . shanties, of course, weather-browned boards, unpainted and often even unplanned, rudely nailed together, sides and roof of the same material, as incapable of keeping out wind and rain as so many paper boxes."

Leland's hotel and the iron pier are shown in an image from *The Illustrated American* of August 30, 1890. The drawing reflects an often written about, but vanished physical characteristic of the beach, its high bluff. Where is the former bluff? An extensive segment of the northern tip of Sandy Hook is an accretion made over many years of tidal action washing away the shore and sending the sand north.

Carriages meeting the evening train could produce a traffic jam on Ocean Avenue. This scene in front of the United States Hotel appeared in *Appleton's Magazine* in 1872.

Cranmer's (typically pronounced without the "n") Pavilion, near the pier on the west side of Ocean Avenue, was one of Long Branch's most popular swimming locales.

The casino and gas tank dominate this undated photograph of the beach and Ocean Avenue taken from the pier. (Collection of Karen L. Schnitzspahn.)

The casino and convention hall, built in 1907, housed a variety of events.

Meyer Goldberg of Chicago built this stadium on the Ocean Avenue block between South Broadway and Laird Street, the locale of the former Ocean Hotel, as a site for greyhound racing in 1934. It was an exciting, but short-lived sport, put out of business the next year by a court ruling. The dogs chased a mechanical rabbit, typically running quarter-mile races, which took about 27 seconds, with ten races each night. (Collection of John Rhody.)

Following the ban on dog betting, midget automobiles raced in the pre-WW II years, succeeded by stock cars after the war. Car racing was a dirty, messy operation that fell into disrepute after a number of seasons. The stadium was demolished at an unspecified date. The entrance to the pier is at lower left. Note the Garfield Memorial in front of the grandstand. See p.111. (The Dorn's Collection.)

The team of the Phil Daly Hose Company Number 2, seen in 1914, is pulling their engine past the pavilion at Broadway and Ocean Avenue. The company, organized in April 1886, was proud of its speed in responding.

Max's beachfront hot dog stand opened in 1928, attracting a following that gave it legendary status. The product's size and "special secret" flavoring were especially appealing, enhanced by the waterfront locale, since hot dogs in American lore are made to be consumed at ball parks and outdoor events. The boardwalk fixture suffered a 1984 fire and was moved to its present location at Ocean Boulevard and Matilda Terrace.

Heavy rains had dampened coastal Monmouth in early September 1944, but the area had been spared hurricane force winds until the middle of that month when a fierce storm, including massive waves, smashed the shore that had still not recovered from a 1943 beating. It washed away and crushed much in its path. The remains of the merry-go-round suggest the storm's force, which buckled the boardwalks and sent the Chelsea pavilion into the waves. (Collection of John Rhody.)

The City of Long Branch built Ocean Park in 1905, south of South Broadway, on the site of the former Ocean Hotel. The 10-acre park, decorated with flower beds and fountains, featured a bandstand, the site of popular concerts. This postcard image is dated c. 1905. (Collection of John Rhody.)

Palm trees were planted to create an exotic look, but local conditions are not conducive to their survival. Some shore areas now install new ones repeatedly, but Long Branch's are gone. This June 1979 photograph is of Ocean Avenue looking south.

Huyler's was a popular Ocean Avenue ice cream stand run by New York candy manufacturer John S. Huyler. It is seen in a 1901 photograph by William Jackson, a fine Classical Revival White House look-alike design.

The Metropolitan Hotel, a large L-shaped structure on the northwest corner of Ocean and Cooper Avenues, was built c. 1854. Its expansive lot extended to the New Jersey Southern railroad tracks and a station on the edge of its grounds. The Metropolitan was owned and run at various times by legendary Long Branch hotel names, including Coopers, Vandykes, and Samuel Laird. (Schenck *Album of Long Branch*.)

The Metropolitan, renamed the Brighton, endured through modern times. Seen on this c. 1910 postcard, their 1920 hotel guide advertisement called themselves "The modern hotel on the sea shore," with "bath houses, a dancing pavilion, large lawns . . ." That size would appear to be a reduction from the larger structure at top. The National Guard building, now vacant, was erected on this site.

The Ocean House has the appearance of a small hotel, which it was while located at the northern end of Ocean Avenue prior to relocation south of Mansion House and conversion into stores. According to Schenck, it contained a notions store, pharmacy, and Richard Van Houton's saloon, "a well ordered and quiet resort, where palatable liquors are dispensed to the thirsting ones . . . " Really?

The staff at the Ocean Hotel is correct in posing in apparent military formation, as military precision was probably needed to feed its army of diners. This photograph was taken c. 1873.

Mansion House, seen in this *c.* 1867 image in a much-expanded state, was built as the Morris House in 1846, reportedly the second oldest boarding house in Long Branch. Samuel Laird bought it in 1852, giving it the better-known name, adding the south wing, and remodeling the place. (Schenck *Album of Long Branch.*)

The United States Hotel was built on Ocean Avenue, south of Chelsea Avenue in 1852 by F. Kennedy and his associates, George and Isaac Crater. Samuel Laird bought the place in 1868, which he operated in conjunction with the Mansion House, a hotel he had owned for many years. This image is from *c.* 1867. A parking lot and vacant arcades fill the site today. (Schenck's *Album of Long Branch.*)

The Atlantic Hotel, located at Ocean and Morris Avenues, seen in a *c.* 1907 postcard, was destroyed by a tragic fire in 1925. Three persons were killed, including two firemen who fell with a collapsing roof and an 18-year-old waitress. After initially escaping, she returned to collect possessions and was trapped in the burning building.

The new Atlantic Hotel was built in 1926, replacing the one at top. The new structure was of substantial brick construction, reflecting newer codes. This image is a *c.* 1930s postcard. Details of its removal were not available. A motel is on the site today.

The Jules S. Abecasis house stood on Ocean Avenue, between North Bath and Pavilion Avenues. The Second Empire house, built c. 1870, had an unusual double-sided mansard. This incredible survivor still stands, sided and missing most of its decorative trim, including the two dormers at top. (Collection of Long Branch Public Library.)

SCARBORO HOTEL, LONG BRANCH, N. J.

The Scarboro Hotel, on Ocean Avenue at South Bath Avenue, became the city's largest following a series of expansions, readily seen on this c. 1910 postcard. Sea View Towers is on the site now. (Collection of John Rhody.)

The Vendome-Plaza was one of the new hotels built in the late 1920s as the Long Branch shore showed signs of vigor during a prosperous era. (The Dorn's Collection.)

The core of Howland's Hotel, Ocean Avenue near Brighton Avenue, was the c. 1828 Sayrs House. Henry Howland bought the place after two interim owners, making various enlargements and remodelings over his long tenure. He was a native of the area and had several business and public interests. The Howland primarily drew a Philadelphia trade. The hotel, vacant for several years, was destroyed by fire in December 1912. Howland Avenue was cut through the site now occupied by apartments and townhouses. (Schenck *Album of Long Branch*.)

The enormous Continental Hotel had its origins as the 1827 National Hotel, built as a "farm house," to which another building was added to create the North Hotel. It was renamed and rebuilt under Samuel Cooper's ownership as the Cooper House. C.C. Sprague and H.A. Stokes, who bought the place in 1866, constructed the central portion, absorbing as wings the National Hotel on the north and, another hotel, Congress Hall, on the south, then renaming the expanded complex, the Continental Hotel. (Schenck *Album of Long Branch*.)

The Ocean Hotel had imported water from Saratoga, New York and other mineral springs, offering "Congress Water" as an enhancement of service to guests. After their suppliers stopped shipping, realizing they were aiding a distant competitor, the Ocean proprietor tapped local springs, calling their water "Congress Hall Water," reasoning a section actually had been Congress Hall. Thus, they found a local solution to the battle of the waters, while their theater company was performing *Much Ado About Nothing*.

The Stetson House, built in 1867 at the northwest corner of Ocean and Brighton Avenue, was a "smaller," 300-room L-shaped structure. The location was long the site of hotels, including the 1832 Lawn House. Charles A. Stetson Jr.'s hotel aimed for a higher-level clientele, but it foundered financially until sold and enlarged in 1873. It was then known as the West End Hotel, which was demolished in 1906. Garden apartments are on the site today. (Schenck *Album of Long Branch*.)

The West End Cottages were built *c.* 1880 on the southeast corner of Ocean and Brighton Avenues, opposite the Pennsylvania Club, as an expansion of the West End Hotel on the northwest corner. The cottages, seen on this *c.* 1910 postcard, survived the 1906 demolition of the hotel until meeting its end at an unspecified date. A major residential development is planned for the site, vacant for some years.

The Takanassee Hotel was built on the site of the demolished West End Hotel in 1906. Although listed in a directory as accommodating 150 guests, the building, with a six-story rear section, appears to have had a larger capacity. For years, it was Long Branch's newest hotel (no other was built until after WW I) but it could not survive the Depression. It was demolished in the 1930s, reportedly to save real estate taxes. The image is a *c.* 1910 postcard. (Collection of Glenn Vogel.)

"Bellevue" was built *c.* 1864 by famed Philadelphia banker Anthony J. Drexel on the west side of Ocean Avenue between the Stetson and Howland Hotels. It follows traditional forms, stylistically, although the high, steeply pitched dormers suggest the Gothic Revival. (Schenck *Album of Long Branch*.)

John F. Chamberlain built this elaborate Second Empire-style "club house" designed by New York architect and builder John B. Terhune in 1868. The building, located near the southwest corner of Ocean and Brighton Avenues, cost a reported $40,000, an enormous sum then. Chamberlain "discovered" Long Branch on learning that gamblers in his New York gaming house left the city in the summer for the shore. His extensive gambling operations caused the wrath of others in the field, who likely did not regret his forced sale of the club after financial reverses at Monmouth Park. (Schenck *Album of Long Branch*.)

Phil Daly, a noted Philadelphia gambler, bought the Pennsylvania Club, expanding and modernizing it with the support of Richard J. Dobbins. His elite clientele included presidents and noted financiers. This *c.* 1910 postcard image shows the Chamberlain place at left and the later pavilions at right. The club was closed by anti-gambling forces in the early 20th century.

L. Rothenberg's hotel, built in 1901 on the west side of Ocean Avenue, catered to a German clientele. Stores on the ground floor included a well-known pharmacy. The Rothenberg was destroyed by fire in the 1930s. Low-rise stores are on the site today.

The Sand and Surf Hotel at 701 Ocean Avenue, near Cedar Avenue, seen in 1957, was a place of no special distinction prior to its reincarnation as the Harbor Island Spa, a resort with a health and fitness theme. It was quite successful for some years, serving a Jewish clientele, but closed following financial difficulties. The vacant place was demolished in the recent past. A tall apartment house occupies the site today. (The Dorn's Collection.)

United States Life Saving Station Number 5 at 805 Ocean Avenue is a three-building complex now owned by the Takanassee Beach Club and presumably part of its facility. However, when asked shortly prior to publication, the owner replied, "We don't discuss that." Its oldest structure was an 1876 Stick Style design modeled on an example exhibited at that year's Centennial Exposition in Philadelphia. This *c.* 1905 postcard image shows a *c.* 1890s Shingle Style station in the foreground, similar to others built in the area, with a *c.* 1900 boathouse in the rear. (Moss Archives.)

The original photograph of the carriage in front was Alfred D. Vanderbilt's, winner of a 6-mile road race from Sea Bright to Hollywood in 26 minutes time.

The *c.* late 1960s Windmill Restaurant is a fascinating example of roadside vernacular architecture built decades after the peak of its popularity. An attention-grabbing structure reflects the area's change from the magnet-hotels to urban street turned highway. The popularity of the image has resulted in its use as a logo for the restaurant's franchised chain, with other outlets housed in traditional structures.

Paddy Murray's Inn, which opened in 1953, became a neighborhood institution. The traditional tavern was, as one resident recalled, "the type place one would go for his first drink." It is seen on West End Avenue in 1975.

The Hotel Keller was one of several in the Brighton and Pond Avenue area. It was likely built *c*. 1890s. A location a block from Ocean Avenue resulted in a different character and often historical obscurity.

The Hotel Keller was destroyed by fire on July 21, 1909. Red Bank photographer Charles Foxwell was on the scene, printing this photograph on a postcard. It may be the site most distant from Red Bank existing in his postcard oeuvre, making one wonder if he was called to the site or was he merely passing by.

Cedar Avenue past Norwood looking towards the shore in a 1947 image shows a wide boulevard that in time would suggest a road-widening project for the section west of this scene. See page 72. (The Dorn's Collection.)

Takanassee Lake at right, formerly known as Greens Pond, is the traditional separation of West End and Elberon. St. Michael's is barely discernible on its north bank. The first major crossing going from east to west is the New York and Long Branch tracks, while Van Court is the north-south street near the bottom. Norwood is just off the picture. Cedar Avenue is the major east-west street. South of Cedar on the shore, observers can find the Harbor Island Spa (p.99) and the houses that made up the early Redemptorist Retreat House (pps. 104–105). The aerial view was taken December 7, 1961. (The Dorn's Collection.)

The Second Empire-style Jeremiah W. Curtis house may have been the most ornate of the family compound on the east side of Ocean Avenue, south of Cedar Avenue and north of Takanassee Lake. It was probably built c. 1870, with considerable Victorian-era fretwork added to it. The family made their fortune with Mrs. Winslow Soothing Syrup. (Collection of Long Branch Public Library.)

The home of Jeremiah W. Curtis, son of Jeremiah H. Curtis, also Second Empire style, is more restrained in its decorative finish. The property was bought by the Redemptorist Fathers in 1922 for the establishment of a retreat house. (Collection of Long Branch Public Library.)

A 1950 aerial view of the Redemptorist Fathers' place shows the two houses on the opposite page on either side of the one-story building built between them, and a third house on the north, or left. A prayer grotto was built in front of the house at right. The first retreat was held in September 1925. The fathers built a large following after small beginnings. (The Dorn's Collection.)

The Redemptorists' first name, St. Joseph's, was changed in 1925 to San Alfonso, in honor of the founder of their order. The retreats increased considerably, helped by a devoted following of the Knights of Columbus and papal endorsement of the retreat process. The original facilities were outgrown and the houses demolished. A new center was built in 1967–68 and dedicated on September 22, 1968. San Alfonso's is a major retreat center, while their building is a significant spiritual landmark on the New Jersey coast.

St. Michael's Roman Catholic Church, West End, Long Branch, N. J.

The Victorian gothic St. Michael's at 796 Ocean Avenue was designed by James Thornton and John Burke and built by the latter. The building contract was let in July 1883, a basement was completed with a temporary roof installed in 1884, while the cornerstone is dated July 25, 1886. The necessity to raise funds delayed the project, with the church finally dedicated on August 9, 1891. This image is from c. 1905. The cross is no longer on the gable, a statue of the Virgin Mary is in a niche in the gable over the window, the porte cochere was removed and covered entrances were built on the east and north.

James Augustine McFaul, born 1850 near Larne, County Antrim, Ireland, came to New York as an infant, settled in New Jersey as a youth, received spiritual guidance in St. Peter's Church, New Brunswick, and completed theological studies at Seton Hall, being ordained in 1877. After several parish assignments in northern New Jersey, McFaul came to Our Lady Star of the Sea in Long Branch in May 1883 as their third pastor, a tenure marked by the opening of the Star of the Sea Academy (p.67) in 1887 and two mission churches, Precious Blood in Monmouth Beach and St. Michael's in West End. He was transferred to the cathedral in Trenton after seven years, was appointed chancellor of the diocese, and in 1894 was consecrated its second bishop. Rapid expansion marked his tenure, including the establishment of 65 parishes. McFaul died in 1917.

Takanassee Lake at left is the traditional border between West End and Elberon. The large, well-defined lots make this aerial photograph *c.* 1940 comparable to a large-scale map. The circular drive on the shore near the center is the James M. Brown/Stella Maris House (p.108), while adjacent on the right is the Grant cottage (p.109). The large shore front oval at the right denotes the Moses Taylor House (p.112). The dark line across the center is the New York and Long Branch Railroad. (The Dorn's Collection.)

George W. Childs's first summer house was on the west side of Ocean Avenue, adjacent to the Pavilion Hotel. This traditional-style house with intersecting gables was built in 1854 by Jacob Dock, reportedly the second cottage erected on the shore, bought by Childs in 1866 from an interim owner, and later sold to James M. Brown in exchange for the house on the following page. (Special Collections & Archives, Rutgers University Libraries.)

James M. Brown, an immigrant Irish banker who founded the New York branch of Brown Brothers & Company, hired Edward T. Potter of New York to design Sea Cliff Villa, this magnificent Stick Style house, built in 1867–68 at 981 Ocean Avenue. The place is often associated with a later owner, the famed Philadelphia publisher, George W. Childs, but rarely with a third, New York banker Adolph Lewisohn, who probably installed the richly carved paneling, fireplace, and stairs in the main hall. The Sisters of St. Joseph of Peace bought the property in 1941. (Schenck *Album of Long Branch*.)

The Sisters of St. Joseph of Peace bought the Brown/Childs House for $14,000 in 1941, opening a "summer house for Sisters" in 1942. It had a capacity of 30 and was renamed Stella Maris Convent. Two wings were added in 1959. The one on the north is seen in this *c.* 1960s postcard image. Another, not visible, is built on the east, expanding capacity to 75. In 1965, Bishop George W. Ahr granted permission to keep Stella Maris open all year to conduct weekend retreats "for girls who may be good vocation prospects for your Congregation."

Charles W. Clinton of New York designed a fine and important Stick Style residence for Howard Potter adjacent to his Brown Brothers partner's. The house was purchased in 1870 for President Grant with the assistance of three wealthy residents, an action that raised ethics questions. Grant, a regular visitor to Long Branch was instrumental in establishing Long Branch's national stature as a premier summer resort. The house's integrity was marred by a major expansion designed by Emile W. Gravent of New York for 1884 buyers Edward A. and Bertha Price, but it is this later image as seen on this c. 1910 postcard that became fixed as the Grant cottage landmark.

The Grant cottage, in poor condition, had been the center of a major preservation campaign. With the site threatened for use as a nightclub, it was purchased by the Sisters for $63,500 in 1963. The building was demolished in 1964. The Stella Maris retreat center grew, attracting a wide public audience. A new chapel was built on the site in 1994, designed by Englewood architect Myron A. Vigod (although the contractor made changes not authorized by the architect). The ocean as a backdrop enhances the spiritual nourishment of morning Mass in the east-facing chapel, not visible in this photograph of the west elevation.

Lewis B. Brown built the Elberon Hotel in 1876 by having architect Charles F. McKim remodel and expand the Charles G. Francklyn house on the east side of Ocean Avenue, opposite Lincoln Avenue. It attracted a high-tune clientele, its success propelled by President Rutherford B. Hayes's visits. His successor, Garfield, was another regular guest. The place, destroyed by fire in 1914, is seen in a *c.* 1904 postcard. (Collection of Robert W. Speck.)

Charles F. McKim designed Charles G. Francklyn's new house, built in 1876 at the northeast corner of Ocean & Lincoln Avenues, south of the Elberon Hotel. This forerunner of the Shingle Style had an asymmetrical arrangement of rooms and verandas around the central hall. This *c.* 1910 image is the west elevation; the ocean side living room contained a large wall of glass. Note the novel carriage way through the house's interior. The building, forever associated with the death of President Garfield, was damaged in the 1914 Elberon Hotel fire and its remains taken down a few years later.

President James A. Garfield, shot by an assailant in Washington July 2, 1881, lingered there for weeks during an insufferable hot spell. Doctors suggested moving him to a healthier climate, the President agreeing to Long Branch, where he had been a frequent visitor. Charles Francklyn's cottage was the destination. Shortly after a right of way was surveyed on September 5, a crew of nearly 2,000 built overnight a railroad track to the house, seen in the middle of this 1881 image. The President's condition rose and fell during a two-week September span.

Garfield died in Long Branch on September 19, 1881. The long vigil and the hopes of the people established a local emotional tie to his death. A monument was ordered and a cornerstone laid in Ocean Park in September 1907. The 28-foot-wide, 16-foot-high Barre granite structure was made by Thomas J. Manson & Sons of Red Bank. Completion, purchase of a seven-foot statue, and the dedication were delayed until 1918, when a reported crowd of 25,000 witnessed a parade and ceremony on September 2. The well-weathered statue by J. Otto Schweizer, Swiss born, European trained, Philadelphia sculptor, is seen in this c. 1960s image looking towards Ocean Avenue. It was moved adjacent to the boardwalk c. 1990 and stands in front of the Ocean Place Hilton Hotel in a new Presidential Park, commissioned by the Long Branch Historical Association and dedicated in July 1997. (Special Collections & Archives, Rutgers University Libraries.)

The Moses Taylor House, designed by Charles Follen McKim in 1876, was built the next year at 1063 Ocean Avenue. Its expression of 18th-century motifs make it a magnificent example of the development of American domestic architecture. Taylor (1806–1882) was a major banker and capitalist, notably with utilities and the Delaware, Lackawanna and Western Railroad. The house was demolished in the early 1980s, the period this image was taken.

This c. 1905 Pach photograph may at first appear to be a remodeling, with the architect inserting every Colonial Revival motif he knew. It is the Elberon Isador Straus house, built in 1901 and designed by James and Leo of New York. The rectangular plan and side gables suggest new Colonial Revival construction, but the decoration is unrestrained. Straus was a part-owner of Macy's; the architect also designed one of the New York Macy stores. The land, bought from the Elberon Improvement Co., was actually in Deal, reflecting imprecise use of the popular Elberon name. The house was demolished, perhaps around the time of its 1925 sale to Shoreland Development Corp. (Collection of Karen L. Schnitzspahn.)

The Castlewall mansion was built in 1888, its name stemming from the tower at left. (Collection of Robert W. Speck.)

James W. Gerard (1794–1874) was a New York lawyer and active reformer for treatment of youthful offenders. He bought a part of the old Woolley farm in 1866 from William M. Gawtry, and built in 1867 this early Second Empire-style house, a virtual transition from Stick Style. Located at the northeast corner of Ocean and Park Avenues, he called the place "Sand Souci." The summer dwelling, made to appear larger by its wide porches, communicated with its nearby coach house via an early system of signal bells. (Schenck *Album of Long Branch*.)

The Elberon Casino, designed by Boston's Peabody and Stearns, was built in 1883 at the northeast corner of Lincoln and Elberon Avenues. Casinos, in their 19th-century parlance an upper-class social club, were built in several popular areas appealing to the wealthy, including Short Hills, New Jersey. A large, general lounging room was in the section at left, while an auditorium was behind the side gables at right. (Collection of Long Branch Public Library.)

THORNE HEDGE, HOME OF F. HOUSMAN, ELBERON, N. J.

The Casino, remodeled as a private home, is depicted on this c. 1940 postcard when it was the residence of F. Housman. The place maintained its exterior integrity in the remodeling. Porches were enclosed, an interior chimney added on the north, and ivy was permitted to grow rampant. The building survived until 1959, when it was destroyed for the construction of several new houses. (Collection of Robert W. Speck.)

The 1899 Elberon Railroad Station at Lincoln Avenue, described stylistically in its National Register nomination as Queen Anne-Richardsonian Romanesque, was one of the most artistic on the New York and Long Branch line. Its rock face stone is obscured in this c. 1905 postcard by its massive hip-gambrel roof. A substantial 60 percent of its ground space was taken up by the open colonnaded area. This station, having replaced an earlier one lost to a fire, was also destroyed by fire in May 1988.

This Shingle Style with Colonial Revival modifications house at 111 Lincoln Avenue was built in 1878 and designed by Charles Follen McKim of McKim Mead and Bigelow, the work dating a year prior to Stanford White's joining the firm. The firm had an active shore practice, but much of that work was destroyed, making this house a rare survivor, a status perhaps attributable to manageable size and location off the coast.

Charles T. Cook, president of Tiffany & Company, New York, built his summer cottage at 20 Lincoln Avenue in 1885. The rear of his lot adjoined the St. James Chapel (p.117 bottom). The architects were McKim, Mead, and White, with the plans probably drawn by Charles F. McKim, in view of the absence of Stanford White during the project. Roth comments on the house's lack of fluidity of form and surface that later characterized the firm's shingled work.

Louis Long bought the house at 988 Elberon Avenue in 1905, one of unspecified origin, on property owned by Daniel and Mary Lyddy since 1887. He immediately made Classical Revival additions and alterations designed by Lansing G. Holden and built by I.R. Taylor of Asbury Park. The house still appears similar to this c. 1906 image from Taylor's office monograph.

The Elberon Memorial Presbyterian Church at 70 Park Avenue was built in 1886 with funds provided by Moses Taylor's widow as a memorial to him. The fine, shingled Gothic Revival edifice is an outstanding example of ecclesiastical architecture of its time. The church contains its original Hilbourne Roosevelt-built pipe organ and maintains an outstanding music program during the summer. No substantive information to identify the architect exists, assertions to the contrary by the church notwithstanding.

The Church of the Presidents, the popular name of the St. James Chapel, was built in 1879 at 1260 Ocean Avenue, to preclude the necessity of Elberon country cottagers having to travel to the Episcopalian church on Broadway. Noted New York architects Potter and Robertson designed the Shingle Style edifice. A 15-foot addition to the chancel (the square tower) was made in 1893, designed by John Snook & Sons of New York. The Long Branch Historical Museum organization acquired the building in 1953, and operated it as a museum for years. However, the site, which was listed on the National Register in 1976, has been closed recently and is in a deplorable state of decline that threatens the building's survival. (Special Collections & Archives, Rutgers University Libraries.)

Martin Beck, the noted New York theatrical figure, had a summer home at 1028 Elberon Avenue. The house is well preserved, maintaining this appearance from a c. 1912 postcard.

Residence of M. Dittman, Elberon, N. J.

The Elberon residence of Marie Dittman is seen on a c. 1910 postcard. The house stands at 69 Brighton Avenue in Deal, once known informally, in part, as South Elberon. This location indicates how far south "Elberon" was used. The house's few changes include a door in place of the bay window.

Later Elberon area homes reflect the revival styles popular in the early 20th century. The J. Edgar Thomson House at the right shows Tudor influence, while the unidentified one at left is a massive, gambrel-roofed Colonial Revival. They are seen on this *c.* 1910 postcard image. The street, likely and extensively changed Ocean Avenue, may be south of the Long Branch border.

Tile-roofed, stucco-clad Italian Renaissance Revival houses were popular throughout eastern Monmouth County in the early decades of the 20th century. Herman Cohn probably built his *c.* 1905 at a nearby location, perhaps outside Elberon proper.

Gustavus W. Pach, born 1845 in Berlin, began photography in Long Branch in 1862 after an apprenticeship with the Appletons of New York. He was joined by his brother Gotthelf, left, in the Long Branch business, and by a second brother, Oscar, a business manager for the firm in New York, for this *c.* 1890 photograph. Pach Brothers earned a national reputation, particularly as portraitists. Headquartered in New York, they established several branch offices, including one at nearby Ocean Grove, and another at a former New Jersey winter resort town, Lakewood. Gustavus died in New York in 1904. (Collection of Long Branch Public Library.)

Pach, who began his Long Branch career out of a cigar store, fitted a wagon for field work in 1867, photographing many of the fine houses, churches, and hotels along the Long Branch shore and environs. A large collection of prints were pasted by hand in the book *Album of Long Branch: A Series of Photographic Views with Letter-Press Sketches* by J.H. Schenck, published in 1868, from which this volume draws liberally. In 1867, Pach built and opened a gallery in the rear of the north wing of the Continental Hotel. This image appears to be a later gallery.

Four

A FEW LONG BRANCH PEOPLE

Elene Hicks, born in 1902 and a graduate of Star of the Sea Academy, entered the 1923 competition for Miss Long Branch at a carnival for celebrating a newly paved Ocean Avenue. She surprised herself and won, the unanimous choice of the judges. She represented Long Branch in that year's Miss America pageant in Atlantic City, during a period when entrants represented cities, rather than the states, as they do now. She is front center, number 49, surrounded by smiling, but unidentified companions. The photograph was lent by a proud, pleased daughter, Elene Eager Dwyer.

A sizable construction crew is seen at an unidentified project in Long Branch in an early 20th-century image. The crew is not well organized in rows, but one worker can be identified, William Hayden, in the back, to the left of the hand of the man standing over the rest.

Anna Mabel Hayden is attractively dressed in early 20th-century summer attire.

A cute Helen Bradley Juska appears as if she could be enveloped by the fur collar and muff. She appears slightly apprehensive, perhaps over the presence of the photographer. After a retail career, a retired Mrs Juska still lives in Long Branch.

The girl in the center, rear, appears to head an unidentified group of locals whose still, dour expressions do not match their appealing attire, c. 1900.

Clarkson S. Fisher, born in Long Branch in 1921 and a veteran of WW II, was educated at Notre Dame and its law school, graduating the latter in 1950. He practiced in Long Branch with Juska and Fisher prior to appointment to the Monmouth County bench in 1964. Fisher was appointed judge of the New Jersey Superior Court in 1966 and to the United States District Court in 1970, serving as chief judge from 1979 to 1987 and as senior judge (for him, a change of status, but not hours worked) from 1987 until shortly prior to his death in 1997. Fisher's elected service included the West Long Branch Borough Council and the New Jersey Assembly. A tireless advocate for adequate Federal courts, the building in Trenton is named in his honor. Clarkson was, in the words of one of his clerks, "brilliant, a great, great judge, with few having had the trust and affection he received."

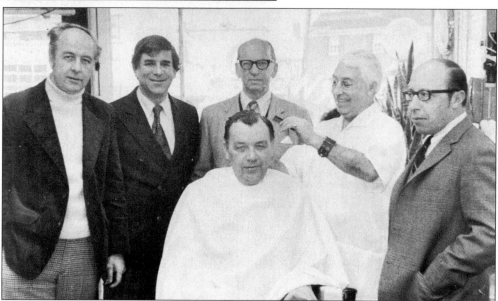

"How did your husband manage to get his picture taken in a barber shop?" asked the author Mae Fisher. "He was always being followed by someone with a camera then." Clarkson Fisher is seen receiving a trim from Ben, the barber, c. 1970s. Others are, from left, William Throckmorton, a Long Branch lawyer, Samuel Teicher of the Teicher Agency, Edward F. Juska, Fisher's law partner, and Henry Cioffi, a Long Branch mayor.

Joseph Paul Kiernan, known by his middle name, a three-sport athlete at Chattle High School and one of this century's major Long Branch public figures, began government work with a county undersheriff position in the 1930s. He was elected to the Long Branch Board of Commissioners in 1940, holding various Democratic party posts over the years and was elected Monmouth County sheriff in 1965, re-elected four times, losing a bid for a sixth term in 1980. Paul Kiernam served two terms as Long Branch Mayor, served on the county board of taxation and the state Law Enforcement Planning Agency. Kiernan was remembered as a gentleman and a tireless public servant who maintained his touch for reaching the ordinary person, when he died in 1989 at age 82.

The 12 Acerra brothers of Laurel Street are arguably the most distinguished brother act in baseball history. The family team, began playing in 1938 against Holy Family in Red Bank and endured through 1952. Their accomplishments attracted wide attention, including Ripley's "Believe It or Not," and commemoration in baseball's Hall of Fame. Ten of 11 survivors gathered (most remained in Long Branch) for a reunion in 1978. They are from left to right: (kneeling) Robert, William, Fred, Richard, and Louis; (standing) Joseph, Paul, Alfred, Charles, and James. Anthony was deceased and Edward not present.

The Phil Daly Hose Company (see p.86) was a well-attired group in their dress uniforms in 1911. They are, from left to right: George H. VanWinkle, Patrick Wells, John Heldt Jr., Charles N. White, Joseph Kingsland, Capt. Frank M. Campbell, Wilbur Lloyd, James Ennis Sr., George Miller, Henry Widdis, Andy Hoag, Joe Schwark, Gary Bodine, Louis Vetter, John Kirby Jr., Philip Schmidt, Philip Eager, Raymond Fesler, David Beach, Harry Heidt, Edward J. Miller, John E. Leonard, and William Connors.

Three committee members are seen in a December 1980 image preparing a time capsule to celebrate the 100th anniversary of the Trinity AME Church at 64 Liberty Street. They are, from left to right, Mrs. Elsie B. Netter, Mrs. Rita Gaton, and Mrs. Mattie Johnson. The capsule contained photographs of church members, copies of their bulletin, hymn books, church laws, and various other memorable items.

The Long Branch High School Class of 1938 is seen at its 30th reunion celebration at the Old Orchard Country Club. Clarkson S. Fisher is the tenth in the third row. The class president, Dr. Reissner, is also in the third row.

Lauren "Woody" Woods is seen directing the noted actor Broderick Crawford. (Tova Navarra photograph.)

Lillie Langtry (nee Emile Charlotte Le Breton), 1853–1929, was popularly known as "The Jersey Lily" from her native Isle of Jersey, England. She married Edward Langtry, visiting on a yacht in 1874, using her very good looks to carry her into London society and a later career as "a professional beauty." Lillie became an actress after separating from her husband in 1881, but was better known for her liaisons, including an extended affair with Edward, Prince of Wales. Her success on the stage, based on shocking the public, made her rich. Lillie was a frequent visitor to Long Branch, usually in the company of wealthy boyfriends. No image of her nude bathing escapade in Pleasure Bay was available, so this discreet portrait from the 1880s appears.

A skeletal denizen of the pier's Haunted Mansion is seen tapping out the notes in 1978. The author expects his book, if not the closing figure, is well fleshed out. Presumably, Ossie here, returned to dust, literally, in the 1987 fire that destroyed the pier, ending a link to one of the glories of Long Branch's storied past.

Hochstetler

101 Words to Know

Black Beauty

ISBN-13: 978-0-545-03332-9
ISBN-10: 0-545-03332-2

12 11 10 9 8 7 6 5 4 3   8 9 10 11 12/0

Printed in the U.S.A.
First printing, November 2007

Book design by Jennifer Rinaldi Windau

101 Words to Know

Black Beauty

by Anna Sewell

Adapted by Joanne Mattern

SCHOLASTIC INC.

New York Toronto London Auckland Sydney
Mexico City New Delhi Hong Kong Buenos Aires

Get ready for 4th grade with

101 Words to Know

Learning vocabulary words by reading them

in context is the best way to retain their meaning.

Adapted from the original story for young readers, 101 words you

need to know by the 4th grade are in bold throughout the book.

Also on the page are the definitions of those words. No need to flip

back for definitions; no need to look them up in the dictionary. It's

easy to learn new vocabulary words while

reading a timeless classic!

TABLE OF CONTENTS

CHAPTER 1:
My First Home

My first **memories** are of a large, rolling meadow with a pond of clear water. Apple trees hung over the pond, making a pleasant shady area. At one end of the **meadow** was a forest of fir trees. At the other end was a fast-running brook. I lived in this meadow with my mother. Her name was Duchess. Our **original** master was Farmer Grey, and he was a good, kind man. Anytime my mother saw him, she would trot up to the gate and neigh with joy.

My mother and I spent all our time together. Because

memories (n.)—thoughts of events that happened in the past
meadow (n.)—a large, open field
original (adj.)—first

I could not eat grass when I was very little, I drank my mother's milk. During the day, I ran by her side. At night, I slept close beside her. When it was hot, we stood by the pond, under the shady trees. When it was cold, we had a warm shed to shelter in.

In time, I became old enough to eat grass and my mother went out to work during the day and came back in the evening. I was free to play with the other **colts** in the meadow. There were six other young colts. They were older than I was, but we had great fun together. We would gallop around and around the field as fast as we could. Sometimes our play turned rough, and we would

colt (n.)—a young male horse

bite and kick each other.

One day, my mother was watching our wild play. She **whinnied** to call me away from the others. "I want you to listen to me," she said when I trotted over. "The other colts are good, but they have not learned any manners. You are well-bred. Your **relations** were fine racehorses. You should never kick or bite. I hope you will grow up to be gentle and good. Always work to the best of your **ability**, no matter what happens."

I nodded. I never forgot my mother's words.

whinny, whinnied (v.)—to neigh quietly
relations (n.)—relatives; people in the same family
ability (n.)—the power to do something

CHAPTER 2:
Breaking In

I grew into a **handsome** horse. My coat was fine and soft and shiny black. I had one white foot, a white star on my forehead, and a tiny white patch on my back.

When I was four years old, a man named Squire Gordon came to see me. He looked me all over. He felt each leg and lifted each hoof. He looked at my eyes and inside my mouth. Then he watched me trot and gallop.

"He will make a fine horse, once he has been broken in," Squire Gordon said.

Breaking in! I knew what that meant, and the words

handsome (adj.)—good-looking

frightened me. That meant I would have to learn to wear

a saddle and a bridle and carry a rider on my back. I

would learn to take a rider's commands. I would also

learn to wear a **harness** and pull a cart. I would learn

that I must always do my master's will and not my own,

no matter how **weary** or hungry I was. Being broken in

could be **difficult**.

But Farmer Grey took charge of my breaking in and

he did it so gently that I was not frightened. However,

some things were not at all **agreeable**. I think the worst

thing was having the bit put into my mouth. A bit is

a cold piece of iron that fits between your teeth and

harness (n.)—a set of leather straps and metal pieces that connect
a horse to a carriage
weary (adj.)—worn out; very tired
difficult (adj.)—hard
agreeable (adj.)—pleasing; likable

your tongue. It is held there by straps that go over your head, under your throat, and around your nose and chin so there is no way you can shake it off. I thought the bit was terrible at first. But I knew that my mother always wore one, and so did other grown-up horses. So I learned to wear a bit, too.

I also learned to wear a saddle and a harness. This was not so bad, as my master was gentle and took great care with me. Soon I got used to everything and could do my work as well as my mother did.

For the last part of my training, Farmer Grey would harness my mother and me to a carriage and take us for drives along pleasant country roads. My mother was a good teacher. I soon learned when to go fast or slow and how to pull with her.

My mother talked to me as we rode and gave me a lot

of advice. "There are many kinds of men," she told me one day. "Some are good, like Farmer Grey, but others are **cruel**. A horse never knows who will buy him or what his life will be like. My wish for you is to always do your best and keep up your good name, no matter where you go." She and I both knew that I would have to leave her someday.

cruel (adj.) — mean

CHAPTER 3:
Birtwick Park

In time, I was sent to live at Squire Gordon's **estate**. I was sad to leave my mother and Farmer Grey. I could not speak, of course, but I put my nose into Farmer Grey's hand to say good-bye.

Birtwick Park was a **beautiful** place. I **glimpsed** many fields and woods. The stable held four horses. It had a large window that opened into the yard and let in plenty of fresh air. When I first arrived, I was placed in a stall with some corn to eat. I could look over the sides of the box and see the other horses.

estate (n.)—a large area of land with a house on it
beautiful (adj.)—very pretty
glimpse, glimpsed (v.)—to take a quick look

After I ate, I looked around with **curiosity**. A fat, gray **pony** stood in the stall next to mine. "Hello. What is your name?" I asked.

"I am Merrylegs," he said. "I carry the young ladies on my back. Are you going to live next to me?"

"I think so," I said.

"Well," said the pony, "I hope you do not kick or bite. I do not like a bad neighbor."

Just then, a **chestnut** horse peered over from the stall beyond mine. She was a tall **mare**. Her ears were laid back, and she had an evil look in her eye.

"So it is you who forced me out of my stall," she

curiosity (n.)—the desire to find out about something
pony (n.)—a small horse
chestnut (adj.)—brown
mare (n.)—a female horse

neighed angrily. "How dare you turn a lady out of her own home?"

"I beg your pardon," I said. "I have forced no one out. The man put me here, and I had nothing to do with it. All I want is to live in peace."

"We shall see about that," the mare said with a snort.

Later, when the mare was outside, Merrylegs told me about her. "That's Ginger," he said. "She has a bad **habit** of biting and snapping. She used to snap at me. One day, she bit James, the stable boy, and made his arm bleed. Then the young ladies were afraid to come in here."

"I have never bitten anything but grass," I assured

habit (n.)—a routine way of acting

the pony. "What pleasure could Ginger find in biting people?"

"I don't think she finds pleasure in it," Merrylegs said. "It's just a bad habit. She says no one was ever kind to her, so why shouldn't she bite? Still, she has nothing to complain about here. John and James are the kindest men you will ever meet, and Squire Gordon and his family treat us well."

Soon I was taken out to see Squire Gordon and his family. They seemed very **impressed** with me.

"What a beautiful horse!" cried his daughters.

"He has such a handsome face, and he is such a

impress, impressed (v.)—to make people think highly of someone or something

lovely color!" said Mrs. Gordon. "Why don't we call him

Black Beauty?"

That is how I got my name.

coachman (n.)—a person who guides horses when they are pulling a carriage

spirit (n.)—enthusiasm; a positive state of mind

CHAPTER 4:
Ginger

I was very happy in my new home, and I knew Squire Gordon was happy with me. On my first day there, the **coachman**, John Manly, took me out for a ride. When he came back, Squire Gordon asked how I was.

"First-rate, sir," John replied. "He is as fast as a deer and has a fine **spirit**. The lightest touch of the rein will guide him. He's **steady** as they come, too, and never **hesitates**. It's my **opinion** he was never frightened or badly used. I am quite **satisfied** with him."

After that day, Squire Gordon often took me for rides

---

steady (adj.)—firm; not shaky
hesitates (v.)—to stop before you do something
opinion (n.)—how a person feels about something
satisfy, satisfied (v.)—to be content; please

and used me for special **occasions**. When I was not needed, I was free to **graze** in the pasture. Ginger often grazed with me. We spent a great deal of time talking. I told her all about my early life and my breaking in.

"My life was very different," Ginger said. "No one was ever kind to me. I was taken from my mother as soon as I was **weaned**. The man who took care of us never said a kind word. He was not cruel to us, but he never showed us any **affection** either."

Ginger paused to pull up a mouthful of grass. "Then there were the boys on the footpath. They used to pass through our field and throw stones at us. It made us

occasion (n.)—an event; a time when something special happens
graze, grazed (v.)—to eat grass
wean, weaned (v.)—able to eat regular food instead of its mother's milk
affection (n.)—strong liking or love

wild, trying to dodge their stones."

"How was your breaking in?" I **inquired**.

"Awful. Several men **seized** me and held my head so tightly I could **scarcely** breathe. They forced the bit into my mouth and hit me and pulled me to make me move." Ginger stamped her hoof, as if the memories made her angry. "If I didn't do what my master wanted, I was whipped. It wasn't fair. I was willing to work hard, but what right did anyone have to treat me cruelly?"

I had to agree with her. Our conversation made me more grateful for the pleasant years I'd spent with my mother in Farmer Grey's meadow.

inquire, inquired (v.)—to ask
seize, seized (v.)—to grab with great force
scarcely (adv.)—barely

Another day, Ginger told me about her first master.

"He was a fashionable gentleman in London. He used to ride me with a bearing rein." I looked at her, puzzled, for I had never heard of such a thing. "A bearing rein is **torture**," Ginger explained. "It holds your head so high that you cannot move it at all. I grew wild, bucking and kicking whenever anyone tried to harness me. At last, the gentleman sold me. I had several masters after that. Some were good and some **neglected** me. Finally, I came here to Squire Gordon's."

"He is a kind man and good to his horses," I said. "So why are you still so wild?"

torture (v.)—to cause extreme pain
neglect, neglected (v.)—to not take care of something

"Of course it is agreeable here, but how long will it last? I wish I could have a bright spirit like you do, but I can't after all I've been through."

I felt sorry for Ginger. As the weeks went on, however, she did become more gentle and cheerful. James and John were always kind to her, and she finally began to trust them. I was happy for her, because we became very good friends.

CHAPTER 5:
The Bridge

One day in late autumn, Squire Gordon had to go on a long **journey** for his business. John **hitched** me to a small cart and we set off.

It had rained heavily the night before and the wind was still blowing strongly. We came to a low wooden bridge over the river. The water flowed fast and high under the bridge.

"The river is rising fast," warned the man at the toll gate. "I think things will be very bad, tonight, indeed."

We got to town, and I had a snack and a nice rest

journey (n.)—a trip
hitch, hitched (v.)—to hook up to something

while the master went about his business. His work took longer than expected, so it was very late in the afternoon before we started out for home. By now, the wind was blowing even harder. It was frightening to ride through the woods. The branches whipped and **swayed** overhead and the wind roared. I had never been out in such a bad storm and it made me very nervous. But I remembered what my mother had told me about always doing my best, so I **proceeded** on.

Suddenly, there was a **tremendous** *crack*! A huge oak tree was torn up by the roots, and it fell right across the road. I was frightened, but I did not panic. I stopped

---

sway, swayed (v.)—to move from side to side
proceed, proceeded (v.)—to go forward
tremendous (adj.)—immense

still and waited to see what my master would do.

"That was a close call!" said Squire Gordon. "We can't pass this tree. How will we get to the bridge now?"

"We will have to go back in the other **direction** and take another road. It will make us very late, but it is the only way," John told him.

So we traveled back and around. By the time we got to the bridge, it was nearly dark. We could see that the water was over the middle part of the bridge, but as that had happened before, my master did not worry. I stepped onto the bridge.

As soon as my feet touched the bridge, however, I

direction (n.)—the way someone or something is moving

knew something was wrong. I stopped and would go no farther. "Go on, Beauty!" called Squire Gordon, but I did not **budge**.

John jumped down and held my bridle. He tried to lead me forward but I would not follow. "What's the matter, Beauty?" he asked. Of course, I could not tell him that the bridge was not safe.

Just then a man at the toll gate on the other side ran out of his house. He was waving a torch and shouting **urgently**, "Stop! Stop! The bridge is **shattered** in the middle. The river carried part of it away. If you go on, you'll **plunge** into the river."

---

budge (v.) — to move
urgently (adv.) — demanding immediate attention
shatter, shattered (v.) — to break into many pieces
plunge (v.) — to dive suddenly into water

"Oh, thank you, Beauty!" said John. He patted me on the nose. "I knew something had to be wrong for you to act that way. Thank goodness for your **wisdom**."

Now we had to go even farther out of our way. By the time we reached home it was late and very dark. Mrs. Gordon ran out of the house, crying, "I have been so worried! Were you in an accident?"

"No, but if Black Beauty had not been wiser than we were, it would have been a **disaster**," Squire Gordon told her.

I heard no more, as John led me to the stable. What a good supper he gave me that night! Then I lay down

wisdom (n.)—knowledge
disaster (n.)—an event that causes great damage; something that turns out very wrong

to rest on a thick bed of straw. I was glad of it, for I was very weary.

CHAPTER 6:
Fire!

Not long after the incident at the bridge, Squire

Gordon and his wife decided to visit some friends. The

journey would take nearly two days. Ginger and I were

chosen to pull the carriage.

The first day we traveled thirty-two miles and had

to pull the carriage up some big hills, but James drove

us so carefully that we did not lose our **enthusiasm**.

Ginger was very good company. By now we were quite

fond of each other. We spent the time talking and

sharing stories. It reminded me of the days when I was

enthusiasm (n.)—great excitement or interest

harnessed with my mother.

At sundown, we stopped in a town for the night. Ginger and I were taken to a hotel stable. The **hostler** rubbed us down and put out a fine meal for us in our stalls.

Later that evening, another traveler's horse was brought in. While he was being rubbed down, a young man lounged in the stable door, talking and smoking a pipe.

"I say," said the hostler, "run up into the loft and dump some hay down for this horse, would you? Just lay down your pipe first."

hostler (n.)—a person who takes care of horses at an inn

The other man agreed and did as he was **requested**.

Soon afterward, the door was locked for the night, and I fell asleep.

I do not know how long I slept. I woke up suddenly, feeling very uncomfortable. The air was thick and hard to breathe. I heard Ginger coughing and the other horses moving around restlessly. The stable was so dark I could see nothing. I heard a low, crackling sound. The sound was so strange that it made me tremble all over.

Suddenly, the hostler rushed into the stable. He started untying the horses and trying to lead them outside. But he was so frightened that he **terrified** me

request, requested (v.)—to ask
terrified (v.)—scared

even more. None of the horses would go with him. They were all too scared.

Finally, the hostler came to me. He tried to drag me out by force, but it was no use. "Come on!" he shouted. When he realized none of the horses would budge, he ran outside.

The crackling sound grew louder. Now I could see lights flickering on the far wall. I heard someone outside yell "Fire!" Flames leaped out of the loft and the crackling sound became a violent roar.

I was crazed with fear. Then I heard James's voice. He was quiet and cheerful, as if nothing was wrong. "Come along, Beauty, we must be going now," he said calmly. His soft voice calmed me. I knew I could trust him so I stepped out of my stall. James took off his scarf and tied it over my eyes. Then, he gently coaxed me out of the stable.

As soon as we were safe, James handed me over to someone else and ran back inside. I knew Ginger was still trapped. I let out a frantic whinny as James ran back into the stable. Soon enough, he came out through the smoke, leading Ginger.

"Make way! Make way!" someone shouted. The fire engine clattered into the yard, pulled by two strong horses. As we were led out of the yard, I saw the firemen jump from the carriage and heard the terrified cries of the horses still inside.

James brought Ginger and me to another stable and we were soon settled again for the night. Ginger told me that if she hadn't heard me whinnying outside, she never would have had the courage to follow James.

The next day, the hostler came to talk to James about the disaster. He said no one was sure how the fire had started, but it was thought that the young man had left his pipe in the hayloft. He told James that the roof had fallen in, and all that was left were the black walls. Two poor horses had died.

"I'll say one thing," the hostler said. "Your horses know whom they can trust. It's one of the hardest things in the world to get a horse out of a stable during a fire."

The hostler was right. Ginger and I knew that we could trust James completely. We were both lucky he was there that night.

CHAPTER 7:
Going to the Doctor

The rest of our trip was very pleasant, and we returned home a few days later. Sadly, soon after our return, James was offered a better job at another estate. We were all sorry to see him go. John hired a boy named Joe Green to take his place. Joe was fourteen and eager to learn, but he was small. James joked that it would take six months before he could do the work properly.

One night, I had finished my dinner of hay and was fast asleep when I heard the stable bell. John rushed in

promptly (adv.) —immediately; quickly

and led me out of my stall. "Wake up, Beauty, we need you now more than we ever have," he said. He **promptly** had a saddle on my back and a bridle over my head.

As we came outside, the Squire rushed up to us, a lantern in his hand. "Ride for your mistress's life, John," he said. "Give this note to Doctor White and give your horse a rest at his home. Then come back as soon as you can."

John said, "Yes, sir," and we were off on our **mission**. We rode through the village and across the bridge. A long, straight road lay before us. "Now, Beauty, do your best," John said. For two miles, I galloped as fast as I could. I don't **believe** a racehorse could have run any faster.

mission (n.)—a special job
believe (v.)—to be sure something is true

After an eight-mile run, we arrived in the next town. We thundered up to Doctor White's house. John jumped off my back and pounded at the door. The doctor poked his head out of a window. "What do you want?" he asked.

"Mrs. Gordon is very ill. The master wants you to go at once. She will die if you do not come."

The doctor came downstairs. "I have no horse. One is sick and my son took the other. Can I use yours?"

John frowned. "He has ridden at a gallop nearly all the way, sir, but if that is the only way, then I don't think my master would mind. Take him. I'll walk home."

So the doctor and I galloped off. He was heavier than John and not as good a rider, but I knew Mrs. Gordon was depending on me. Even though I was tired and hot, I ran back the way I had come.

When we got to Birtwick Park, the doctor hurried into the house. Joe led me into the stable. I was never so glad to be home. All I could do was stand and pant. Sweat ran down my legs and clouds of steam rose off my hot body.

Joe did the best he could to help me, but he was still young and untrained. He rubbed my legs and chest but did not put a cloth over me. Then he gave me a pail of cold water to drink and some hay and corn to eat. Thinking he had done all the right things, he left.

Soon I began to tremble. I felt so cold and my body ached all over. How I wanted a warm blanket to cover me! I wished John was there to help me, but he had to walk eight long miles home. All I could do was stand in my stall and shiver.

At last, I heard John at the door. I moaned and he

ran to my side. I could not tell him what was wrong, but

he seemed to know. In an instant, he had covered me

with two warm blankets. Then he mixed warm water

and oats to make gruel. After I drank it, I went to sleep.

"Stupid boy!" I heard him say as I dozed off. "No cloth

put on, and I dare say the water was cold, too." But I

knew Joe had meant well.

I became very sick. I had a fever and an infection

in my lungs. It hurt even to breathe. John nursed me

night and day. Squire Gordon often came to see me, too.

"My poor Beauty," he told me one day. "You saved your

mistress's life, you know." I was very glad to hear that.

Joe Green spent many hours at my side, too. He was

heartbroken over what he had done and told me often

how sorry he was. I forgave him, and in time, John

did, too.

I was ill a long time, but slowly I got better.

Eventually, I was able to join Ginger and Merrylegs

outside and pull the carriage again. Everyone was

happy that I had **recovered**.

recover, recovered (v.)—to get better after an illness or injury

CHAPTER 8:
A New Home

For three years, I lived a happy life with the Gordons.

However, though my friends and I did not know it,

our days at Birtwick Park were coming to an end.

Although there were no more frantic runs to the doctor,

Mrs. Gordon was still very sick. Finally, Doctor White

advised her to leave England and live **abroad**. She

needed to move to a warmer **climate** to save her health.

"I hate to sell off the house and all the horses,"

Squire Gordon told John, "but there is nothing else I can

do." He told John he had sold Ginger and me to his old

abroad (adv.)—in another country
climate (n.)—the usual weather in a place

friend, the Earl. Merrylegs was given to the minister, who wanted a pony for his wife. Joe would go to take care of him. I knew **loyal** Squire Gordon had done his best for us.

The next morning, Ginger and I were hitched to the carriage and brought to the **vast** lands of Earlshall Park. For the most part, Ginger and I were happy there. We were well fed and looked after by men who knew how to care for horses. Still, something was missing. "I don't feel the people around us are our friends," Ginger said one day. I knew exactly what she meant.

One person at Earlshall Park was definitely not our

loyal (adj.)—faithful
vast (adj.)—huge

friend. That was the Earl's wife. Whenever we drove her, she demanded that the coachman place Ginger and me in a bearing rein so we would look **elegant**. I had never worn a bearing rein because Squire Gordon thought it was cruel. I soon found out he was right.

The first time Ginger and I were hitched to the carriage, our reins were pulled so tight that we could not move our heads up or down. The arrangement was not just uncomfortable, it made it impossible for us to use all our **strength**. Whenever we went up a hill, pain shot through my back and legs.

"Now you see what I was talking about," Ginger told

elegant (adj.) — graceful and stylish
strength (n.) — power; toughness

me after we had arrived back home. "Today the reins were not too bad. But if they make them any tighter, I won't take it!"

Our reins grew shorter and tighter each day as York, the coachman, tried to get us used to the bearing rein. Finally, a few weeks later, the Earl's wife said sharply, "Really, York, I've had enough of this nonsense. These horses are not fit to be seen. Raise their heads at once!"

York grumbled, but he did as he was told. He fixed my reins so tight, I could hardly bear it. Ginger saw what was coming. As York walked to her side, she reared up suddenly and knocked him flat. She kept rearing and kicking until several servants ran out to hold her still.

We had no ride that day. Ginger and I were taken back to the stable. She was never put into the carriage harness again. Instead, the Earl gave Ginger to his son to use as a hunter. I was paired up with another horse named Max to pull the carriage. Max was used to the bearing rein, so he did not complain.

I had to suffer the bearing rein for four long months. I am sure that if it had lasted much longer, either my health or my **temper** would have been destroyed. People said I looked high-spirited and elegant, but they had no idea how much pain I was in.

Finally, the Earl and his whole family went away for a long visit. That was a pleasant time. Ginger and I and some other horses were left at home. Most of the time, we were just used for riding, so there was no need for the bearing rein.

temper (n.) —disposition; state of feeling

Chapter 9:
A Terrible Accident

While the Earl was away, I and the other horses

were left in the care of Reuben Smith, the head **groom**.

Reuben **possessed** fine skills as a horseman. He could

drive a carriage as well as anyone. He cared for the

horses as well as a **veterinarian** and almost as well as a

veterinary **surgeon**. All of us horses liked him.

There was just one thing wrong with Reuben. He

loved to drink whisky. Most of the time he was fine, but

every now and then he would drink so much, he would

disgrace himself. The Earl had even fired Reuben once,

groom (n.)—a person who cares for horses
possess, possessed (v.)—to own
veterinarian (n.)—a doctor who treats animals
surgeon (n.)—a doctor who performs operations

but York had begged the Earl to take the man back. The Earl did, but only after Reuben promised he would never drink again.

Reuben kept his promise. Then, one night while the Earl was away, he broke it. Reuben had ridden me to town on some business, and while he was there, he got very drunk. When he came to pick me up from the stable, the hostler told him that one of the nails in my front shoes was coming loose. "No matter," Reuben said. "It will be all right until we get home."

I was surprised, for Reuben was usually very careful about our shoes. Still, what could I do? I started for home. I soon realized that Reuben was drunk and in a very bad mood. **Perhaps** he had **quarreled** with someone.

Reuben rode me at a hard gallop. He even used the

whip to urge me to go faster, though I was already going as fast as I could. Riding so hard over the rough road, my shoe became even looser. It wasn't long before it fell off. If Reuben had been paying attention, he would have realized that something was wrong with my pace, but he didn't notice.

Past the toll gate there was a long stretch of road on which sharp stones had just been laid. No horse could **navigate** the road quickly without risking danger, but Reuben would not slow my pace. In no time, my hoof was broken and split, and the inside of my foot was terribly cut by the sharp stones.

perhaps (adv.)—maybe
quarrel, quarreled (v.)—to have an argument
navigate (v.)—to travel through a difficult area

No horse could keep his footing under these circumstances. **Suddenly**, I stumbled and fell hard on both of my knees. Reuben was flung off my back. Because I was going so fast, he was **launched** with great force. I **staggered** to the side of the road and waited. In the moonlight, I could see Reuben lying in the road. He groaned once or twice, and then lay still.

Hours passed. Finally, two men came along on horseback and stopped to help, but it was too late for Reuben. He was dead.

In time, my injured foot and shattered knees healed, but the doctor said the scars on my legs would never

suddenly (adv.)—unexpected
launch, launched (v.)—to send something flying into the air
stagger, staggered (v.)—to walk unsteadily

fade. I was no longer fit for the Earl's stables, so I was put up for sale.

Ginger was sorry to see me go. "You're my only friend," she said. "We'll probably never see each other again."

CHAPTER 10:
Horse for Rent

York **recommended** me to a man who ran a **livery** stable. He knew the man was always looking for good horses and that he took good care of them. The sale was arranged, and I left Earlshall Park for good.

My new life was very different. In the past, I had always been driven by people who knew what they were doing. In this place, however, I was rented out to whomever would pay for me. I soon **observed** that there were many different kinds of people.

recommend, recommended (v.)—to suggest something is good or worthwhile

livery (n.)—a stable where horses are rented out for work

observe, observed (v.)— to watch carefully

Some were tight-rein drivers. These men seemed to think that they should hold the reins as tight as they could, always pulling on the horse's mouth. Other drivers held the reins too loosely and had no control over the horse. I could not depend on these drivers for **guidance** or **encouragement**.

The worst drivers were those who thought horses were machines. It made no difference to these drivers if the road was rocky or muddy, or how heavy my load was. They were determined to get their money's worth from me. So even though I struggled to do my best, they would whip me and call me a lazy beast.

guidance (n.)—advice or direction
encouragement (n.)—praise

I lived here for several months. Then I was taken

to a horse fair and sold again. Here I was poked and

prodded by many people. They looked at my teeth and

checked my legs. They always looked at my scarred

knees. Then I would hear them say that I might stumble

and fall easily, so I could not be trusted. If only I could

have explained what had really happened!

Finally, at the end of the day, two men came up to me.

One was loud and unpleasant. I hoped he would not buy

me. The other had a kind voice and spoke gently. I could

tell by the way he handled me that he knew a lot about

horses. Finally, the kind man made the final offer. That

was how my life as a London cab horse began.

prod, prodded (v.)—to poke or jab

CHAPTER 11:
The Streets of London

My new master's name was Jerry Barker. Jerry called me Jack. The next day, he put me into the cab. Jerry took great pains to be sure my collar and bridle fit comfortably. There was no bearing rein! Then we drove to the cabstand where Jerry worked. The stand had a number of iron rails. Cabs were drawn up all along the rails. The horses whinnied softly to each other while the drivers read the newspaper or talked as they waited for their next fare.

My first week as a cab horse was very difficult. I had never been to London, and all the noise and crowds frightened me at first. But I soon got used to it. Jerry was as good a driver as I had ever known. He never laid the whip on me. Soon we were able to understand each other as well as a horse and a man can. We also had every Sunday off. We worked so hard during the week that we both needed that day of rest. Jerry and his family took great care of me. I always had good food to eat and was well groomed every morning and evening. It was a great treat to be talked to and pet again. I did my best to let them know that I appreciated their kindness.

One day, while Jerry and I waited at the cabstand for a fare, a **shabby** old cab horse drove up beside us. She was a worn-out **wreck**, with her bones showing through her thin coat. I was shocked at the hopeless look in her

shabby (adj.)—worn or neglected
wreck (n.)—something that is destroyed

eyes, and I thought that I had seen this horse before.
Then she turned and stared at me. "Black Beauty, is
that you?" she asked.

It was Ginger! How she had changed! I moved closer
so she could tell me her story.

The Earl's son had used her for a hunter until she
was worn out. Then she was sold to a gentleman. Things
went well for a while, but then she was sold again and
again. Each time her **situation** got worse. Finally, she
was **purchased** by a livery stable and rented out to
different drivers.

"You look well off, and I am glad of it," Ginger told

situation (n.)—circumstances; the way things are at a particular time
purchase, purchased (v.)—to buy

me. "I cannot tell you how hard my life has been. They whip me and work me hard, without a thought of how I suffer."

"You used to stand up for yourself when you were treated badly," I said.

"I did once, but what's the use?" she replied. "Men are stronger than horses. If they are cruel, there is nothing we can do."

I felt terrible **grief** for her. I could say nothing to **comfort** her, just put my nose up to hers. But I think she was pleased to see me, for she said, "You are the only friend I ever had."

grief (n.)—terrible sadness
comfort (n.)—being happy and safe

Then Ginger's driver came up and pulled her out of line. They drove off. I felt terribly sad.

CHAPTER 12:
My Final Home

I hoped to work for Jerry for a long time, for I liked
him. However, my time with him was **brief**. Around New
Year's Eve, our long hours in the bitter cold got the better
of Jerry. He became very ill and had to stay in bed.

When Jerry got well, his family decided that being a
cab driver was too hard for him. They sold the cab and
me and moved to the country. I went from owner to
owner, and my troubles **increased**. Eventually, I became
a London cab horse again. My new owner was a horrible
man. He whipped me all the time, even though I didn't

brief (adj.)—short
increase, increased (v.)—to grow in size or number

deserve it. "Hurry up, you stupid beast!" he would yell as I **strained** to pull a heavy load up a hill. "Move faster or I'll beat you!" he **threatened**.

One day, I was loaded more heavily than usual. My passengers were a family with a young daughter named Grace. "Papa, that horse is too **weak** to carry us and our bags," she told her father.

"Don't you worry," said the driver as he whipped me. "My horse is strong enough."

"No, the horse can't stand it!" Grace cried. "It's cruel!"

"Grace, the man knows his horse," her father said. "Be quiet!"

---

deserve (v.)—to earn something because of the way you behave
strain, strained (v.)—to put forth a great effort and stress
threaten, threatened (v.)—to make someone feel that they are in danger
weak (adj.)—not strong

I started off and did all right until we came to a hill. I simply did not have the strength to make it any farther. "Come on, you stupid horse!" my driver yelled as he beat me with his whip.

Suddenly, my feet slipped out from under me, and I fell on my side. I lay there for what seemed like a long time. All around me I heard voices shouting. Finally, someone threw cold water on my head and placed a blanket over me. Another man helped me up and led me to a stable.

I was no longer fit for cab work. I was taken to the horse fair to be sold again. This time I was placed with the old and broken-down horses. We were a sorry-looking lot. The buyers and sellers were not in much better **condition** than we were.

People didn't have much use for a horse that could

not do any hard work, so no one wanted to buy me. It was late in the afternoon when I saw a young boy and an older man walk toward me. "Look at this horse, Grandpa," the boy said. "Do you think he was once a carriage horse?"

"Indeed I do, Willie," said the man. "He must have been a fine animal when he was young. He is still very handsome."

"Grandpa, why don't you buy him? Remember Ladybird? She was an old horse, and you made her young again. I bet you can do the same with this one."

The old man laughed. "I can't make all old horses

condition (n.)—the general state of a person or an animal

young," he said.

"This horse isn't old at all," said the salesman. "He's just had a hard time of it. I think plenty of good food and rest and care will make him a fine horse again."

The old man looked me over more carefully then. His touch was **thorough** but so gentle and kind that I nuzzled him and let out a soft whinny to **express** my feelings.

"See, Grandpa, he wants to come with us!" Willie cried. "Please!"

The boy continued to plead, and finally, he convinced his grandfather to buy me. I now belonged to Mr.

thorough (adj.)—careful and complete
express (v.)—to show emotion

Thoroughgood and Willie.

I moved into a large meadow with a comfortable shed for my stable. Mr. Thoroughgood brought me hay and oats every night and morning. I did not have to work. All I had to do was rest and eat and build up my strength.

Willie visited me every day. He often brought me a carrot or some other treat to eat. Sometimes he just stood and watched me eat. He always had a kind word and a gentle pat for me.

Soon I began to feel quite young again. In the spring, Mr. Thoroughgood hitched me to a small carriage. He and Willie drove me for a few miles and were very pleased with me. My legs were not stiff anymore, and I did the work easily.

"By summer he will be as good as Ladybird," Mr.

Thoroughgood said.

Summer came. One day, Mr. Thoroughgood said
it was time to find a good, quiet home for me. Not
long after that, I was cleaned and groomed. I knew
something special was about to happen. I was hitched
to the carriage, and Willie and his grandfather drove
me a few miles away. We pulled up in front of a pretty
house set in a beautiful meadow.

"I hope the ladies like him," said Mr. Thoroughgood
as he stepped down from the carriage.

The ladies were Miss Blomefield, Miss Lavinia, and
Miss Ellen. They looked me over carefully. "I can tell
you that there is no horse more gentle and willing to
work than this one," Mr. Thoroughgood told them.

"He is a beauty," said Miss Ellen.

"Yes, but look at his knees," said Miss Blomefield.

She pointed to my scars. "He's fallen once. What if he falls again? I should never get over the fright."

"Many fine horses have had their knees broken because their drivers were **careless**," Mr. Thoroughgood said in **explanation**. "I'm **certain** that is what happened to him."

"You have always given us good advice," Miss Blomefield said. "I want our coachman to have a look at him."

Willie ran to the stables and **emerged** with a handsome young man. He looked at me very carefully. He touched the white star on my forehead. "I once

---

careless (adj.)—not careful
explanation (n.)—the reason for something
certain (adj.)—sure
emerge, emerged (v.)—to come out of

knew a horse that looked exactly like this," he said in surprise. "This horse has the same white star and one white foot. And—oh my goodness!—here is the patch of white hair on his back. This must be Black Beauty!"

I stared at the young man in surprise. "Oh, Beauty, do you remember me? I'm Joe Green. I was the stable boy who almost killed you." He began patting me as if he were overjoyed.

I have to admit I didn't recognize Joe at all. He had been just a boy when I had seen him last, but now he was a big, strong man.

"Oh, Beauty, I can see you've had a hard time of it. I promise you shall have nothing but good times now." He turned to the three women. "Ladies, I beg you to take this **opportunity** and buy this horse. You'll never see a finer animal."

The ladies smiled. I knew I had found a happy home at last.

I have been here for a year now. Everyone is kind to me, and my work is easy and pleasant. Willie comes to visit me whenever he can. The ladies promise that I will never be sold, so I have nothing to fear. This is my **permanent** home.

Still, there are times in the early morning, before I am fully awake, when I dream I am back at Squire Gordon's, talking with Ginger and Merrylegs under the shade of the apple trees.

opportunity (n.)—chance
permanent (adj.)—meant to last for a long time

PUZZLES

Word Maze

Can you find the hidden vocabulary word in each of these puzzles? Start with the boxed letter. Draw a line from each correct letter to the next—up, down, across, or diagonal—to reveal the word. Not all letters are used.

```
Y [S] T Z        J U [E] R        [B] L V R
H A P L          D S T I          U E P D
D M I Y          U Q A C          L N O M
H R I E          X V T B          I V M F
Q F P T          B E H G          E A E K
```

S _ _ _ _ _   E _ _ _ _ _ _   B _ _ _ _ _ _ _

Carriage Horse Jumble

Unscramble these letters to find words
that have to do with horses.

SNREHAS

MOROG

YNIWNH

IELVYR

NACMOAHC

ZRGAE

A Message from Black Beauty

Use the code to figure out the secret message. Substitute the correct letter for each number in the puzzle. You'll come up with an important message from Black Beauty.

CODE:

A=24	G=22	M=12	S=15	Y=10
B=3	H=5	N=21	T=6	Z=14
C=26	I=16	O=23	U=17	
D=1	J=9	P=2	V=8	
E=20	K=18	Q=25	W=19	
F=7	L=11	R=4	X=13	

<u>2</u> <u>20</u> <u>23</u> <u>2</u> <u>11</u> <u>20</u>   <u>15</u> <u>5</u> <u>23</u> <u>17</u> <u>11</u> <u>1</u>

<u>21</u> <u>23</u> <u>6</u>   <u>3</u> <u>20</u>   <u>26</u> <u>4</u> <u>17</u> <u>20</u> <u>11</u>

<u>6</u> <u>23</u>   <u>5</u> <u>23</u> <u>4</u> <u>15</u> <u>20</u> <u>15</u>.

A Twisted Tale

Use the words in the box to fill in the missing word in each sentence. Then unscramble the circled letters to find a word that describes Black Beauty and fill in the sentence.

shattered   urgent   disaster   memories

mission   temper   chestnut   terrified

Black Beauty's friend Ginger was
a _ (_) _ _ _ _ _ _ mare.

Squire Gordon sent John and Black Beauty
on an important _ _ _ _ _ (_).

It was _ _ _ (_) _ _ that they fetch the doctor.

Black Beauty and Ginger were
_ _ _ _ _ _ _ _ (_) during the fire.

If Black Beauty had crossed the bridge, it would have been a _ _ _O_ _ _ _.

Ginger had a bad _ _O_ _ _.

Black Beauty fell andO_ _ _ _ _ _ _ _ his knees.

Black Beauty had both good and bad _ _ _O_ _ _ of his life.

Black Beauty was a _ _ _ _ _ _ _ _ horse.

Saddle Up Word Search

Can you find these words from the story in the puzzle?
Look across, up, down, and diagonally.

abroad   prod   affection   recover
budge   **steady**   **glimpse**   **strength**
neglect   **weak**   **plunge**   **wreck**

```
A  W  D  J  P  R  O  D  B  Q
B  G  T  N  B  E  D  N  E  L
R  R  A  F  B  U  N  E  D  R
O  I  O  G  G  S  D  C  H  V
A  R  C  L  W  K  P  G  O  L
D  K  L  I  P  R  U  A  E  W
T  Q  U  M  L  O  E  R  A  S
C  C  Z  P  R  U  M  C  R  T
E  P  X  S  I  V  W  Z  K  E
L  O  C  E  P  Y  E  C  B  A
G  H  B  E  I  A  A  O  H  D
E  Z  V  U  A  S  K  X  S  Y
N  H  I  R  E  C  O  V  E  R
A  F  F  E  C  T  I  O  N  H
G  F  Q  E  P  L  U  N  G  E
E  R  S  T  R  E  N  G  T  H
```

Who Am I?

Write the word from the box next to its definition.
When you're finished, the first letter of each word
will spell the name of someone in the story.

| emerge | launch | impress | loyal | inquire | wean |

_ _ _ _   to eat regular food instead of mother's milk

_ _ _ _ _ _ _   to ask

_ _ _ _ _ _   to send into the air

_ _ _ _ _   faithful

_ _ _ _ _ _ _   to cause someone to think highly of you

_ _ _ _ _ _   to come out of

A boy who loved Black Beauty: _ _ _ _ _ _

Wheels of Synonyms

Each carriage wheel has a word missing. Read all the synonyms in each wheel. Find the word that fits. Write it in the empty space.

difficult   weary   vast   quarrel   loyal   beautiful

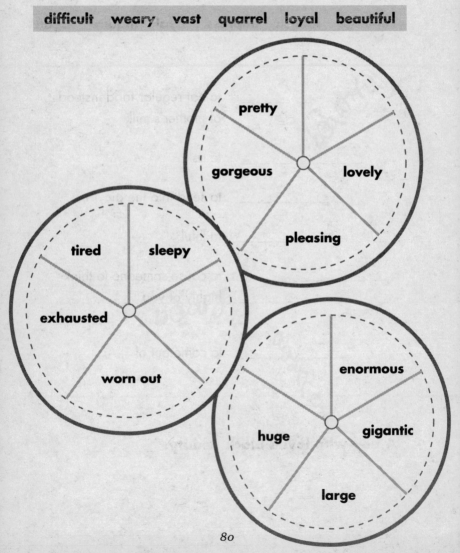

pretty

gorgeous   lovely

pleasing

tired   sleepy

exhausted

worn out

enormous

huge   gigantic

large

80

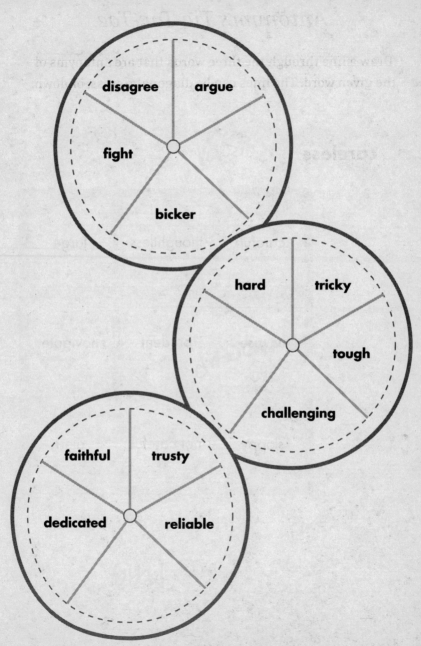

Antonyms Tic-Tac-Toe

Draw a line through the three words that are antonyms of the given word. The lines can be diagonal, across, or down.

careless

careful	thoughtless	large
unwise	prudent	navigate
sloppy	not careful	alert

cruel

kind	nasty	brief
pleasant	unkind	harsh
merciful	elegant	mean

grief

sorrow	pain	misery
woe	unhappiness	prod
bliss	joy	delight

Vocabulary Words

noun (n.), verb (v.), adverb (adv.), adjective (adj.)

ability (n.)—the power to do something

abroad (adv.)—in another country

affection (n.)—strong liking or love

agreeable (adj.)—pleasing; likable

beautiful (adj.)—very pretty

believe (v.)—to be sure something is true

brief (adj.)—short

budge (v.)— to move

careless (adj.)—not careful

certain (adj.)—sure

chestnut (adj.)—brown

climate (n.)—the usual weather in a place

coachman (n.)—a person who guides horses when they are pulling a carriage

colt (n.)—a young male horse

comfort (n.)—being happy and safe

condition (n.)—the general state of a person or an animal

cruel (adj.)—mean

curiosity (n.)—the desire to find out about something

deserve (v.)—to earn something because of the way you behave

difficult (adj.)—hard

direction (n.)—the way someone or something is moving

disaster (n.)—an event that causes great damage; something that turns out very wrong

elegant (adj.)—graceful and stylish

emerge, emerged (v.)—to come out of

encouragement (n.)—praise

enthusiasm (n.)—great excitement or interest

estate (n.)—a large area of land with a house on it

explanation (n.)—the reason for something

express (v.)—to show emotion

glimpse, glimpsed (v.)—to take a quick look

graze, grazed (v.)—to eat grass

grief (n.)—terrible sadness

groom (n.)—a person who cares for horses

guidance (n.)—advice or direction

habit (n.)—a routine way of acting

handsome (adj.)—good-looking

harness (n.)—a set of leather straps and metal pieces that connect a horse to a carriage

hesitates (v.)—to stop before you do something

hitch, hitched (v.)—to hook up to something

hostler (n.)—a person who takes care of horses at an inn

impress, impressed (v.)—to make people think highly of someone or something

increase, increased (v.)—to grow in size or number

inquire, inquired (v.)—to ask

journey (n.)—a trip

launch, launched (v.)—to send something flying into the air

livery (n.)—a stable where horses are rented out for work

loyal (adj.)—faithful

mare (n.)—a female horse

meadow (n.)—a large, open field

memories (n.)—thoughts of events that happened in the past

mission (n.)—a special job

navigate (v.)—to travel through a difficult area

neglect, **neglected** (v.)—to not take care of something

observe, **observed** (v.)— to watch carefully

occasion (n.)—an event; a time when something special happens

opinion (n.)—how a person feels about something

opportunity (n.)—chance

original (adj.)—first

perhaps (adv.)—maybe

permanent (adj.)—meant to last for a long time

plunge (v.)—to dive suddenly into water

pony (n.)—a small horse

possess, **possessed** (v.)—to own

proceed, **proceeded** (v.)—to go forward

prod, prodded (v.)—to poke or jab

promptly (adv.) —immediately; quickly

purchase, purchased (v.)—to buy

quarrel, quarreled (v.)—to have an argument

recommend, recommended (v.)—to suggest something is good or worthwhile

recover, recovered (v.)—to get better after an illness or injury

relations (n.)—relatives; people in the same family

request, requested (v.)—to ask

satisfy, satisfied (v.)—to be content; pleased

scarcely (adv.)—barely

seize, seized (v.)—to grab with great force

shabby (adj.)—worn or neglected

shatter, shattered (v.)—to break into many pieces

situation (n.)—circumstances; the way things are at a particular time

spirit (n.)—enthusiasm; a positive state of mind

stagger, staggered (v.)—to walk unsteadily

steady (adj.)—firm; not shaky

strain, strained (v.)—to put forth a great effort and stress

strength (n.)—power; toughness

suddenly (adv.)—unexpected

surgeon (n.)—a doctor who performs operations

sway, swayed (v.)—to move from side to side

temper (n.) —disposition; state of feeling

terrified (v.)—scared

thorough (adj.)—careful and complete

threaten, threatened (v.)—to make someone feel that they are in danger

torture (v.)—to cause extreme pain

tremendous (adj.)—immense

urgently (adv.)—demanding immediate attention

vast (adj.)—huge

veterinarian (n.)—a doctor who treats animals

weak (adj.)—not strong

wean, weaned (v.)—able to eat regular food instead of its mother's milk

weary (adj.)—worn out; very tired

whinny, **whinnied** (v.)—to neigh quietly

wisdom (n.)—knowledge

wreck (n.)—something that is destroyed

Puzzle Answers:

Word Maze

SPIRIT

ESTATE

BELIEVE

Carriage Horse Jumble

HARNESS

GROOM

WHINNY

LIVERY

COACHMAN

GRAZE

A Message from Black Beauty

PEOPLE SHOULD NOT BE CRUEL TO HORSES.

A Twisted Tale

Black Beauty's friend Ginger was a C H E S T N U T mare.

Squire Gordon sent John and Black Beauty on an important M I S S I O N.

It was U R G E N T that they fetch the doctor.

Black Beauty and Ginger were T E R R I F I E D during the fire.

If Black Beauty had crossed the bridge, it would have been a D I S A S T E R.

Ginger had a bad T E M P E R.

Black Beauty fell and S H A T T E R E D his knees.

Black Beauty had both good and bad M E M O R I E S of his life.

Black Beauty was a <u>HANDSOME</u> horse.

Saddle Up Word Search

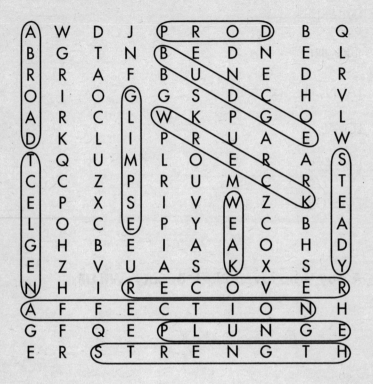

Who Am I?

WEAN

INQUIRE

LAUNCH

LOYAL

IMPRESS

EMERGE

A boy who loved Black Beauty: WILLIE

Wheels of Synonyms

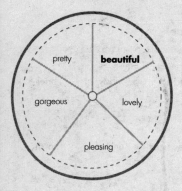

pretty · **beautiful** · gorgeous · lovely · pleasing

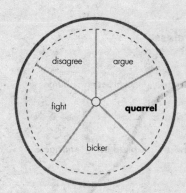

disagree · argue · fight · **quarrel** · bicker

tired · sleepy · exhausted · **weary** · worn out

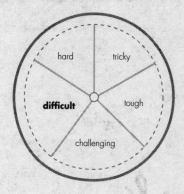

hard · tricky · **difficult** · tough · challenging

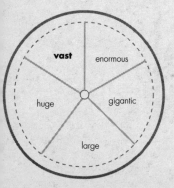

vast · enormous · huge · gigantic · large

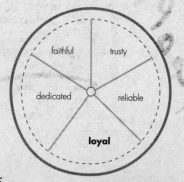

faithful · trusty · dedicated · reliable · **loyal**

Antonyms Tic-Tac-Toe

careless

careful	thoughtless	large
unwise	**prudent**	navigate
sloppy	not careful	**alert**

cruel

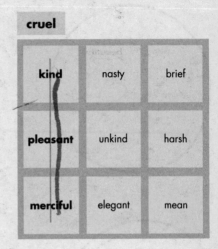

kind	nasty	brief
pleasant	unkind	harsh
merciful	elegant	mean

grief

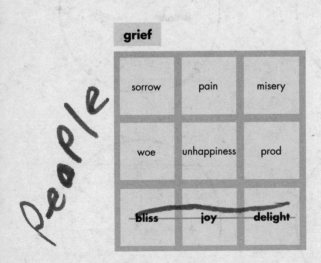

sorrow	pain	misery
woe	unhappiness	prod
bliss	joy	delight

people